LAW, LEGISLATION AND LIBERTY

Volume 1
RULES AND ORDER

LAW, LEGISLATION AND LIBERTY

*A new statement of the liberal principles
of justice and political economy*

Volume I

RULES AND ORDER

F. A. Hayek

The University of Chicago Press

The University of Chicago Press, Chicago 60637
Routledge & Kegan Paul Ltd, London EC4V 5EL
© 1973 by F. A. Hayek. All rights reserved
Published 1973
International Standard Book Number: 0–226–32080–4
Library of Congress Catalog Card Number: 73–82488
Printed in Great Britain by W & J Mackay Ltd

Intelligent beings may have laws of their own making;
but they also have some which they never made.
(Montesquieu, *De l'Esprit des lois*, I, p. i)

CONTENTS

CONTENTS

PREFACE

This volume is the first of three between which I have found it expedient to divide the treatment of the large subject indicated by the general title. According to the plan of the whole sketched in the Introduction, it is to be followed by a second volume dealing with 'The Mirage of Social Justice' and a third treating 'The Political Order of a Free Society'. Since drafts of these further volumes are in existence I hope to be able to bring them out in the near future. The reader who is curious to know where the argument leads will in the meantime find some indication in a number of preliminary studies published during the long years when this work was in preparation and collected partly in my *Studies in Philosophy, Politics and Economics* (London and Chicago, 1967) and more fully (but in German) in my *Freiburger Studien* (Tübingen, 1969).

It would be impossible here to enumerate and thank all who have assisted me in various ways during the ten years this work has occupied me. But there is one obligation which I must specifically acknowledge. Professor Edwin McClellan of the University of Chicago has again, as on an earlier occasion, taken great trouble to make my exposition more readable than I myself could have done. I am deeply grateful for this sympathetic effort but should add that, since the draft on which he worked has since undergone further changes, he must not be held responsible for whatever defects the final version may have.

INTRODUCTION

There seems to be only one solution to the problem: that the élite of mankind acquire a consciousness of the limitation of the human mind, at once simple and profound enough, humble and sublime enough, so that Western civilisation will resign itself to its inevitable disadvantages.

G. Ferrero*

When Montesquieu and the framers of the American Constitution articulated the conception of a limiting constitution[1] that had grown up in England, they set a pattern which liberal constitutionalism has followed ever since. Their chief aim was to provide institutional safeguards of individual freedom; and the device in which they placed their faith was the separation of powers. In the form in which we know this division of power between the legislature, the judiciary, and the administration, it has not achieved what it was meant to achieve. Governments everywhere have obtained by constitutional means powers which those men had meant to deny them. The first attempt to secure individual liberty by constitutions has evidently failed.

Constitutionalism means limited government.[2] But the interpretation given to the traditional formulae of constitutionalism has made it possible to reconcile these with a conception of democracy according to which this is a form of government where the will of the majority on any particular matter is unlimited.[3] As a result it has already been seriously suggested that constitutions are an antiquated survival which have no place in the modern conception of government.[4] And, indeed, what function is served by a constitution which makes omnipotent government possible? Is its function to be merely that governments work smoothly and efficiently, whatever their aims?

In these circumstances it seems important to ask what those founders of liberal constitutionalism would do today if, pursuing

I

the aims they did, they could command all the experience we have gained in the meantime. There is much we ought to have learned from the history of the last two hundred years that those men with all their wisdom could not have known. To me their aims seem to be as valid as ever. But as their means have proved inadequate, new institutional invention is needed.

In another book I have attempted to restate, and hope to have in some measure succeeded in clarifying, the traditional doctrine of liberal constitutionalism.[5] But it was only after I had completed that work that I came to see clearly why those ideals had failed to retain the support of the idealists to whom all the great political movements are due, and to understand what are the governing beliefs of our time which have proved irreconcilable with them. It seems to me now that the reasons for this development were chiefly: the loss of the belief in a justice independent of personal interest; a consequent use of legislation to authorize coercion, not merely to prevent unjust action but to achieve particular results for specific persons or groups; and the fusion in the same representative assemblies of the task of articulating the rules of just conduct with that of directing government.

What led me to write another book on the same general theme as the earlier one was the recognition that the preservation of a society of free men depends on three fundamental insights which have never been adequately expounded and to which the three main parts of this book are devoted. The first of these is that a self-generating or spontaneous order and an organization are distinct, and that their distinctiveness is related to the two different kinds of rules or laws which prevail in them. The second is that what today is generally regarded as 'social' or distributive justice has meaning only within the second of these kinds of order, the organization; but that it is meaningless in, and wholly incompatible with, that spontaneous order which Adam Smith called 'the Great Society', and Sir Karl Popper called 'the Open Society'. The third is that the predominant model of liberal democratic institutions, in which the same representative body lays down the rules of just conduct and directs government, necessarily leads to a gradual transformation of the spontaneous order of a free society into a totalitarian system conducted in the service of some coalition of organized interests.

This development, as I hope to show, is not a necessary consequence of democracy, but an effect only of that particular form of unlimited government with which democracy has come to be identified. If I am right, it would indeed seem that the particular form of representative government which now prevails in the Western world, and which many feel they must defend because they mistakenly regard it as the only possible form of democracy, has an inherent tendency to lead away from the ideals it was intended to serve. It can hardly be denied that, since this type of democracy has come to be accepted, we have been moving away from that ideal of individual liberty of which it had been regarded as the surest safeguard, and are now drifting towards a system which nobody wanted.

Signs are not wanting, however, that unlimited democracy is riding for a fall and that it will go down, not with a bang, but with a whimper. It is already becoming clear that many of the expectations that have been raised can be met only by taking the powers of decision out of the hands of democratic assemblies and entrusting them to the established coalitions of organized interests and their hired experts. Indeed, we are already told that the function of representative bodies has become to 'mobilize consent',[6] that is, not to express but to manipulate the opinion of those whom they represent. Sooner or later the people will discover that not only are they at the mercy of new vested interests, but that the political machinery of para-government, which has grown up as a necessary consequence of the provision-state, is producing an impasse by preventing society from making those adaptations which in a changing world are required to maintain an existing standard of living, let alone to achieve a rising one. It will probably be some time before people will admit that the institutions they have created have led them into such an impasse. But it is probably not too early to begin thinking about a way out. And the conviction that this will demand some drastic revision of beliefs now generally accepted is what makes me venture here on some institutional invention.

If I had known when I published *The Constitution of Liberty* that I should proceed to the task attempted in the present work, I should have reserved that title for it. I then used the term 'constitution' in the wide sense in which we use it also to describe the state of fitness of a person. It is only in the present book that I address myself to the question of what constitutional arrangements, in the legal sense, might be most conducive to the preservation of individual freedom. Except for a bare hint which few readers will have noticed,[7] I confined myself in the earlier book to stating the principles which the existing types of government would have to follow if they wished to preserve freedom. Increasing awareness that the prevailing institutions make this impossible has led me to concentrate more and more on what at first seemed merely an attractive but impracticable idea, until the utopia lost its strangeness and came to appear to me as the only solution of the problem in which the founders of liberal constitutionalism failed.

Yet to this problem of constitutional design I turn only in volume 3 of this work. To make a suggestion for a radical departure from established tradition at all plausible required a critical re-examination not only of current beliefs but of the real meaning of some fundamental conceptions to which we still pay lip-service. In fact, I soon discovered that to carry out what I had undertaken would require little less than doing for the twentieth century what Montesquieu had done for the eighteenth. The reader will believe me when I say that in the course of the work I more than once despaired of my ability to come even near the aim I had set myself. I am not speaking here of the fact that Montesquieu was also a great literary genius whom no mere scholar can hope to emulate. I refer rather to the purely intellectual difficulty which is a result of the circumstance that, while for Montesquieu the field which such an undertaking must cover had not yet split into numerous specialisms, it has since become impossible for any man to master even the most important relevant works. Yet, although the problem of an appropriate social order is today studied from the different angles of economics, jurisprudence, political science, sociology, and ethics, the problem is one which can be approached successfully only as a whole. This means that whoever undertakes such a task today cannot claim professional competence in all the fields with which he has to deal, or be acquainted with the specialized literature available on all the questions that arise.

Nowhere is the baneful effect of the division into specialisms more evident than in the two oldest of these disciplines, economics and law. Those eighteenth-century thinkers to whom we owe the basic conceptions of liberal constitutionalism, David Hume and Adam Smith, no less than Montesquieu, were still concerned with what some of them called the 'science of legislation', or with principles of policy in the widest sense of this term. One of the main themes of this book will be that the rules of just conduct which the lawyer studies serve a kind of order of the character of which the lawyer is largely ignorant; and that this order is studied chiefly by the economist who in turn is similarly ignorant of the character of the rules of conduct on which the order that he studies rests.

The most serious effect of the splitting up among several specialisms of what was once a common field of inquiry, however, is that it has left a no-man's-land, a vague subject sometimes called 'social philosophy'. Some of the chief disputes within those special disciplines turn, in fact, on differences about questions which are not peculiar to, and are therefore also not systematically examined by, any one of them, and which are for this reason regarded as 'philosophical'. This serves often as an excuse for taking tacitly a position which is supposed either not to require or not to be capable of rational justification. Yet these crucial issues on which not only factual interpretations but also political positions wholly depend, are questions which can and must be answered on the basis of fact and logic. They are 'philosophical' only in the sense that certain widely but erroneously held beliefs are due to the influence of a philosophical tradition which postulates a false answer to questions capable of a definite scientific treatment.

In the first chapter of this book I attempt to show that certain widely held scientific as well as political views are dependent on a particular conception of the formation of social institutions, which I shall call 'constructivist rationalism'—a conception which assumes that all social institutions are, and ought to be, the product of deliberate design. This intellectual tradition can be shown to be false both in its factual and in its normative conclusions, because the existing institutions are not all the product of design, neither would it be possible to make the social order wholly dependent on design without at the same time greatly restricting the utilization of available knowledge. That erroneous view is closely connected with the equally false conception of the human mind as an entity standing outside the cosmos of nature and society, rather than being itself the product of the same process of evolution to which the institutions of society are due.

I have indeed been led to the conviction that not only some of the scientific but also the most important political (or 'ideological') differences of our time rest ultimately on certain basic philosophical differences between two schools of thought, of which one can be shown to be mistaken. They are both commonly referred to as rationalism, but I shall have to distinguish between them as the evolutionary (or, as Sir Karl Popper calls it, 'critical') rationalism on the one hand, and the erroneous constructivist (Popper's 'naïve') rationalism on the other. If the constructivist rationalism can be shown to be based on factually false assumptions, a whole family of schools of scientific as well as political thought will also be proved erroneous.

In the theoretical fields it is particularly legal positivism and the connected belief in the necessity of an unlimited 'sovereign' power which stand or fall with this error. The same is true of utilitarianism, at least in its particularistic or 'act' variety; also, I am afraid that a not inconsiderable part of what is called 'sociology' is a direct child of constructivism when it presents its aims as 'to create the future of mankind' [8] or, as one writer put it, claims 'that socialism is the logical and inevitable outcome of sociology'. [9] All the totalitarian doctrines, of which socialism is merely the noblest and most influential, indeed belong here. They are false, not because of the values on which they are based, but because of a misconception of the forces which have made the Great Society and civilization possible. The demonstration that the differences between socialists and non-socialists ultimately rest on purely intellectual issues capable of a scientific resolution and not on different judgments of value appears to me one of the most important outcomes of the train of thought pursued in this book.

It appears to me also that the same factual error has long appeared to make insoluble the most crucial problem of political organization, namely how to limit the 'popular will' without placing another 'will' above it. As soon as we recognize that the basic order of the Great Society cannot rest entirely on design, and can therefore also not aim at particular foreseeable results, we see that the requirement, as legitimation of all authority, of a commitment to general principles approved by general opinion, may well place effective restrictions on the particular will of all authority, including that of the majority of the moment.

On these issues which will be my main concern, thought seems to have made little advance since David Hume and Immanuel Kant, and in several respects it will be at the point at which they left off that our analyses will have to resume. It was they who came nearer than anybody has done since to a clear recognition of the status of values as independent and guiding conditions of all rational construction. What I am ultimately concerned with here, although I can deal only with a small aspect of it, is that destruction of values by scientific error which has increasingly come to seem to me the great tragedy of our time—a tragedy, because the values which scientific error tends to dethrone are the indispensable foundation of all our civilization, including the very scientific efforts which have turned against them. The tendency of constructivism to represent those values which it cannot explain as determined by arbitrary human decisions, or acts of will, or mere emotions, rather than as the necessary conditions of facts which are taken for granted by its expounders, has done much to shake the foundations of civilization, and of science itself, which also rests on a system of values which cannot be scientifically proved.

ONE

REASON AND EVOLUTION

> To relate by whom, and in what connection, the true law of
> the formation of free states was recognized, and how this
> discovery, closely akin to those which, under the names of
> development, evolution, and continuity, have given a new and
> deeper method to other sciences, solved the ancient problem
> between stability and change, and determined the authority of
> tradition on the progress of thought.
>
> Lord Acton*

Construction and evolution

There are two ways of looking at the pattern of human activities
which lead to very different conclusions concerning both its explanation and the possibilities of deliberately altering it. Of these, one
is based on conceptions which are demonstrably false, yet are so
pleasing to human vanity that they have gained great influence and
are constantly employed even by people who know that they rest
on a fiction, but believe that fiction to be innocuous. The other,
although few people will question its basic contentions if they are
stated abstractly, leads in some respects to conclusions so unwel-
come that few are willing to follow it through to the end.

The first gives us a sense of unlimited power to realize our
wishes, while the second leads to the insight that there are limitations to what we can deliberately bring about, and to the recognition that some of our present hopes are delusions. Yet the effect of
allowing ourselves to be deluded by the first view has always been
that man has actually limited the scope of what he can achieve. For
it has always been the recognition of the limits of the possible which
has enabled man to make full use of his powers. [1]

The first view holds that human institutions will serve human
purposes only if they have been deliberately designed for these
purposes, often also that the fact that an institution exists is evidence of its having been created for a purpose, and always that we

should so re-design society and its institutions that all our actions will be wholly guided by known purposes. To most people these propositions seem almost self-evident and to constitute an attitude alone worthy of a thinking being. Yet the belief underlying them, that we owe all beneficial institutions to design, and that only such design has made or can make them useful for our purposes, is largely false.

This view is rooted originally in a deeply ingrained propensity of primitive thought to interpret all regularity to be found in phenomena anthropomorphically, as the result of the design of a thinking mind. But just when man was well on the way to emancipating himself from this naïve conception, it was revived by the support of a powerful philosophy with which the aim of freeing the human mind from false prejudices has become closely associated, and which became the dominant conception of the Age of Reason.

The other view, which has slowly and gradually advanced since antiquity but for a time was almost entirely overwhelmed by the more glamorous constructivist view, was that that orderliness of society which greatly increased the effectiveness of individual action was not due solely to institutions and practices which had been invented or designed for that purpose, but was largely due to a process described at first as 'growth' and later as 'evolution', a process in which practices which had first been adopted for other reasons, or even purely accidentally, were preserved because they enabled the group in which they had arisen to prevail over others. Since its first systematic development in the eighteenth century this view had to struggle not only against the anthropomorphism of primitive thinking but even more against the reinforcement these naïve views had received from the new rationalist philosophy. It was indeed the challenge which this philosophy provided that led to the explicit formulation of the evolutionary view. [2]

The tenets of Cartesian rationalism

The great thinker from whom the basic ideas of what we shall call constructivist rationalism received their most complete expression was René Descartes. But while he refrained from drawing the conclusions from them for social and moral arguments, [3] these were mainly elaborated by his slightly older (but much more long-lived) contemporary, Thomas Hobbes. Although Descartes' immediate concern was to establish criteria for the truth of propositions, these were inevitably also applied by his followers to judge the appropriateness and justification of actions. The 'radical doubt' which made him refuse to accept anything as true which could not be logically derived from explicit premises that were 'clear and distinct', and therefore beyond possible doubt, deprived of validity all those rules of conduct which could not be justified in this manner. Although Descartes himself could escape the consequences by ascribing such rules of conduct to the design of an omniscient deity, for those among his followers to whom this no longer seemed an adequate explanation the acceptance of anything which was based merely on tradition and could not be fully justified on rational grounds appeared as an irrational superstition. The rejection as 'mere opinion' of all that could not be demonstrated to be true by his criteria became the dominant characteristic of the movement which he started.

Since for Descartes reason was defined as logical deduction from explicit premises, rational action also came to mean only such action as was determined entirely by known and demonstrable truth. It is almost an inevitable step from this to the conclusion that only what is true in this sense can lead to successful action, and that therefore everything to which man owes his achievements is a product of his reasoning thus conceived. Institutions and practices which have not been designed in this manner can be beneficial only by accident. Such became the characteristic attitude of Cartesian constructivism with its contempt for tradition, custom, and history in general. Man's reason alone should enable him to construct society anew. [4]

This 'rationalist' approach, however, meant in effect a relapse into earlier, anthropomorphic modes of thinking. It produced a renewed propensity to ascribe the origin of all institutions of culture to invention or design. Morals, religion and law, language and writing, money and the market, were thought of as having been deliberately constructed by somebody, or at least as owing whatever perfection they possessed to such design. This intentionalist or pragmatic [5] account of history found its fullest expression in the conception of the formation of society by a social contract, first in Hobbes and then in Rousseau, who in many respects was a direct follower of Descartes. [6] Even though their theory was not always meant as a historical account of what actually happened, it was always meant to provide a guideline for deciding whether or not existing institutions were to be approved as rational.

It is to this philosophical conception that we owe the preference which prevails to the present day for everything that is done 'consciously' or 'deliberately', and from it the terms 'irrational' or 'non-rational' derive the derogatory meaning they now have. Because of this the earlier presumption in favour of traditional or established institutions and usages became a presumption against them, and 'opinion' came to be thought of as 'mere' opinion— something not demonstrable or decidable by reason and therefore not to be accepted as a valid ground for decision.

Yet the basic assumption underlying the belief that man has achieved mastery of his surroundings mainly through his capacity for logical deduction from explicit premises is factually false, and any attempt to confine his actions to what could thus be justified would deprive him of many of the most effective means to success that have been available to him. It is simply not true that our actions owe their effectiveness solely or chiefly to knowledge which we can state in words and which can therefore constitute the explicit premises of a syllogism. Many of the institutions of society which are indispensable conditions for the successful pursuit of our conscious aims are in fact the result of customs, habits or practices which have been neither invented nor are observed with any such purpose in view. We live in a society in which we can successfully orientate ourselves, and in which our actions have a good chance of achieving their aims, not only because our fellows are governed by known aims or known connections between means and ends, but because they are also confined by rules whose purpose or origin we often do not know and of whose very existence we are often not aware.

Man is as much a rule-following animal as a purpose-seeking one. [7] And he is successful not because he knows why he ought to observe the rules which he does observe, or is even capable of stating all these rules in words, but because his thinking and acting are governed by rules which have by a process of selection been evolved in the society in which he lives, and which are thus the product of the experience of generations.

The permanent limitations of our factual knowledge

The constructivist approach leads to false conclusions because man's actions are largely successful, not merely in the primitive stage but perhaps even more so in civilization, because they are adapted both to the particular facts which he knows and to a great many other facts he does not and cannot know. And this adaptation to the general circumstances that surround him is brought about by his observance of rules which he has not designed and often does not even know explicitly, although he is able to honour them in action. Or, to put this differently, our adaptation to our environment does not consist only, and perhaps not even chiefly, in an insight into the relations between cause and effect, but also in our actions being governed by rules adapted to the kind of world in which we live, that is, to circumstances which we are not aware of and which yet determine the pattern of our successful actions.

Complete rationality of action in the Cartesian sense demands complete knowledge of all the relevant facts. A designer or engineer needs all the data and full power to control or manipulate them if he is to organize the material objects to produce the intended result. But the success of action in society depends on more particular facts than anyone can possibly know. And our whole civilization in consequence rests, and must rest, on our *believing* much that we cannot *know* to be true in the Cartesian sense.

What we must ask the reader to keep constantly in mind throughout this book, then, is the fact of the necessary and irremediable ignorance on everyone's part of most of the particular facts which determine the actions of all the several members of human society. This may at first seem to be a fact so obvious and incontestable as hardly to deserve mention, and still less to require proof. Yet the result of not constantly stressing it is that it is only too readily forgotten. This is so mainly because it is a very inconvenient fact which makes both our attempts to explain and our attempts to influence intelligently the processes of society very much more difficult, and which places severe limits on what we can say or do about them. There exists therefore a great temptation, as a first approximation, to begin with the assumption that we know everything needed for full explanation or control. This provisional assumption is often treated as something of little consequence which can later be dropped without much effect on the conclusions. Yet this necessary ignorance of most of the particulars which enter the order of a Great Society is the source of the central problem of all social order and the false assumption by which it is provisionally put aside is mostly never explicitly abandoned but merely conveniently forgotten. The argument than proceeds as if that ignorance did not matter.

The fact of our irremediable ignorance of most of the particular facts which determine the processes of society is, however, the reason why most social institutions have taken the form they actually have. To talk about a society about which either the observer or any of its members knows all the particular facts is to talk about something wholly different from anything which has ever existed— a society in which most of what we find in our society would not and could not exist and which, if it ever occurred, would possess properties we cannot even imagine.

I have discussed the importance of our necessary ignorance of the concrete facts at some length in an earlier book[8] and will emphasize its central importance here mainly by stating it at the head of the whole exposition. But there are several points which require re-statement or elaboration. In the first instance, the incurable ignorance of everyone of whom I am speaking is the ignorance of particular facts which are or will become known to somebody and thereby affect the whole structure of society. This structure of human activities constantly adapts itself, and functions through adapting itself, to millions of facts which in their entirety are not known to anybody. The significance of this process is most obvious and was at first stressed in the economic field. As it has been said, 'the economic life of a non-socialist society consists of millions of relations or flows between individual firms and households. We can establish certain theorems about them, but we can never observe all.'[9] The insight into the significance of our institutional ignorance in the economic sphere, and into the methods by which we have learnt to overcome this obstacle, was in fact the starting point[10] for those ideas which in the present book are systematically applied to a much wider field. It will be one of our chief contentions that most of the rules of conduct which govern our actions, and most of the institutions which arise out of this regularity, are adaptations to the impossibility of anyone taking conscious account of all the particular facts which enter into the order of society. We shall see, in particular, that the possibility of justice rests on this necessary limitation of our factual knowledge, and that insight into the nature of justice is therefore denied to all those constructivists who habitually argue on the assumption of omniscience.

Another consequence of this basic fact which must be stressed here is that only in the small groups of primitive society can collaboration between the members rest largely on the circumstance that at any one moment they will know more or less the same particular circumstances. Some wise men may be better at interpreting the immediately perceived circumstances or at remembering things in remote places unknown to the others. But the concrete events which the individuals encounter in their daily pursuits will be very much the same for all, and they will act together because the events they know and the objectives at which they aim are more or less the same.

The situation is wholly different in the Great[11] or Open Society where millions of men interact and where civilization as we know it has developed. Economics has long stressed the 'division of *labour*' which such a situation involves. But it has laid much less stress on the fragmentation of *knowledge*, on the fact that each member of society can have only a small fraction of the knowledge possessed by all, and that each is therefore ignorant of most of the facts on which the working of society rests. Yet it is the utilization of much more knowledge than anyone can possess, and therefore the fact that each moves within a coherent structure most of whose determinants are unknown to him, that constitutes the distinctive feature of all advanced civilizations.

In civilized society it is indeed not so much the greater knowledge that the individual can acquire, as the greater benefit he receives from the knowledge possessed by others, which is the cause of his ability to pursue an infinitely wider range of ends than merely the satisfaction of his most pressing physical needs. Indeed, a 'civilized' individual may be very ignorant, more ignorant than many a savage, and yet greatly benefit from the civilization in which he lives.

The characteristic error of the constructivist rationalists in this respect is that they tend to base their argument on what has been called the *synoptic delusion*, that is, on the fiction that all the relevant facts are known to some one mind, and that it is possible to construct from this knowledge of the particulars a desirable social order. Sometimes the delusion is expressed with a touching naïveté by the enthusiasts for a deliberately planned society, as when one of them dreams of the development of 'the art of simultaneous thinking: the ability to deal with a multitude of related phenomena at the same time, and of composing in a single picture both the qualitative and the quantitative attributes of these phenomena.'[12] They seem completely unaware that this dream simply assumes away the central problem which any effort towards the understanding or shaping of the order of society raises: our incapacity to assemble as a surveyable whole all the data which enter into the social order. Yet all those who are fascinated by the beautiful plans which result from such an approach because they are 'so orderly, so visible, so easy to understand',[13] are the victims of the synoptic delusion and forget that these plans owe their seeming clarity to the planner's disregard of all the facts he does not know.

Factual knowledge and science

The chief reason why modern man has become so unwilling to admit that the constitutional limitations on his knowledge form a permanent barrier to the possibility of a rational construction of the whole of society is his unbounded confidence in the powers of science. We hear so much about the rapid advance of scientific knowledge that we have come to feel that all mere limitations of knowledge are soon bound to disappear. This confidence rests, however, on a misconception of the tasks and powers of science, that is, on the erroneous belief that science is a method of ascertaining particular facts and that the progress of its techniques will enable us to ascertain and manipulate all the particular facts we might want.

In one sense the saying that our civilization rests on the conquest of ignorance is of course a mere platitude. Yet our very familiarity with it tends to conceal from us what is most important in it: namely that civilization rests on the fact that we all benefit from knowledge which we do *not* possess. And one of the ways in which civilization helps us to overcome that limitation on the extent of individual knowledge is by conquering ignorance, not by the acquisition of more knowledge, but by the utilization of knowledge which is and remains widely dispersed among individuals. The limitation of knowledge with which we are concerned is therefore not a limitation which science can overcome. Contrary to a widely held belief, science consists not of the knowledge of particular facts; and in the case of very complex phenomena the powers of science are also limited by the practical impossibility of ascertaining all the particular facts which we would have to know if its theories were to give us the power of predicting specific events. The study of the relatively simple phenomena of the physical world, where it has proved possible to state the determining relations as functions of a few variables that can be easily ascertained in particular instances, and where as a consequence the astounding progress of disciplines concerned with them has become possible, has created the illusion that soon the same will also be true with regard to the more complex phenomena. But neither science nor any known technique[14] enables us to overcome the fact that no mind, and therefore also no deliberately directed action, can take account of all the particular facts which are known to some men but not as a whole to any particular person.

Indeed, in its endeavour to explain and predict particular events, which it does so successfully in the case of relatively simple phenomena (or where it can at least approximately isolate 'closed systems' that are relatively simple), science encounters the same barrier of factual ignorance when it comes to apply its theories to very complex phenomena. In some fields it has developed important theories which give us much insight into the general character of some phenomena, but will never produce predictions of particular events, or a full explanation—simply because we can never know all the particular facts which according to these theories we would have to know in order to arrive at such concrete conclusions. The best example of this is the Darwinian (or Neo-Darwinian) theory of the evolution of biological organisms. If it were possible to ascertain the particular facts of the past which operated on the selection of the particular forms that emerged, it would provide a complete explanation of the structure of the existing organisms; and similarly, if it were possible to ascertain all the particular facts which will operate on them during some future period, it ought to enable us to predict future development. But, of course, we will never be able to do either, because science has no means of ascertaining all the particular facts that it would have to possess to perform such a feat.

There is another related misconception about the aim and power of science which it will be useful also to mention at this point. This is the belief that science is concerned exclusively with what exists and not with what could be. But the value of science consists largely in telling us what would happen if some facts were different from what they are. All the statements of theoretical science have the form of 'if . . . , then . . .' statements, and they are interesting mainly in so far as the conditions we insert in the 'if' clause are different from those that actually exist.

Perhaps this misconception has nowhere else been so important as in political science where it seems to have become a bar to serious consideration of the really important problems. Here the mistaken idea that science is simply a collection of observed facts has led to a confinement of research to the ascertainment of what is. While the chief value of *all* science is to tell us what the consequences would be if conditions were in some respects made different from what they are.

The fact that an increasing number of social scientists confine themselves to the study of what exists in some part of the social system does not make their results more realistic, but makes them largely irrelevant for most decisions about the future. Fruitful social science must be very largely a study of what is *not*: a construction of hypothetical models of possible worlds which might exist if some of the alterable conditions were made different. We need a scientific theory chiefly to tell us what would be the effects if some conditions were as they have never been before. All scientific knowledge is knowledge not of particular facts but of hypotheses which have so far withstood systematic attempts at refuting them.

The concurrent evolution of mind and society: the role of rules

The errors of constructivist rationalism are closely connected with Cartesian dualism, that is with the conception of an independently existing mind substance which stands outside the cosmos of nature and which enabled man, endowed with such a mind from the beginning, to design the institutions of society and culture among which he lives. The fact is, of course, that this mind is an adaptation to the natural and social surroundings in which man lives and that it has developed in constant interaction with the institutions which determine the structure of society. Mind is as much the product of the social environment in which it has grown up and which it has not made as something that has in turn acted upon and altered these institutions. It is the result of man having developed in society and having acquired those habits and practices that increased the chances of persistence of the group in which he lived. The conception of an already fully developed mind designing the institutions which made life in society possible is contrary to all we know about the evolution of man.

The cultural heritage into which man is born consists of a complex of practices or rules of conduct which have prevailed because they made a group of men successful but which were not adopted because it was known that they would bring about desired effects.

Man acted before he thought and did not understand before he acted. What we call understanding is in the last resort simply his capacity to respond to his environment with a pattern of actions that helps him to persist. Such is the modicum of truth in behaviourism and pragmatism, doctrines which, however, have so crudely oversimplified the determining relationships as to become more obstacles than helps to their appreciation.

'Learning from experience', among men no less than among animals, is a process not primarily of reasoning but of the observance, spreading, transmission and development of practices which have prevailed because they were successful—often not because they conferred any recognizable benefit on the acting individual but because they increased the chances of survival of the group to which he belonged.[15] The result of this development will in the first instance not be articulated knowledge but a knowledge which, although it can be described in terms of rules, the individual cannot state in words but is merely able to honour in practice. The mind does not so much make rules as consist of rules of action, a complex of rules that is, which it has not made, but which have come to govern the actions of the individuals because actions in accordance with them have proved more successful than those of competing individuals or groups.[16]

There is in the beginning no distinction between the practices one must observe in order to achieve a particular result and the practices one ought to observe. There is just one established manner of doing things, and knowledge of cause and effect and knowledge of the appropriate or permissible form of action are not distinct. Knowledge of the world is knowledge of what one must do or not do in certain kinds of circumstances. And in avoiding danger it is as important to know what one must never do as to know what one must do to achieve a particular result.

These rules of conduct have thus not developed as the recognized conditions for the achievement of a known purpose, but have evolved because the groups who practised them were more successful and displaced others. They were rules which, given the kind of environment in which man lived, secured that a greater number of the groups or individuals practising them would survive. The problem of conducting himself successfully in a world only partially known to man was thus solved by adhering to rules which had served him well but which he did not and could not *know* to be true in the Cartesian sense.

There are thus two attributes of these rules that govern human conduct and make it appear intelligent which we shall have to stress throughout, because the constructivist approach denies implicitly that it can be rational to observe such rules. Of course in advanced society only some rules will be of this kind; what we want to emphasize is merely that even such advanced societies will in part owe their order to some such rules.

The first of these attributes which most rules of conduct originally possessed is that they are observed in action without being known to the acting person in articulated ('verbalized' or explicit) form. They will manifest themselves in a regularity of action which can be explicitly described, but this regularity of action is not the result of the acting persons being capable of thus stating them. The second is that such rules come to be observed because in fact they give the group in which they are practised superior strength, and not because this effect is known to those who are guided by them. Although such rules come to be generally accepted because their observation produces certain consequences, they are not observed with the intention of producing those consequences—consequences which the acting person need not know.

We cannot consider here the difficult question of how men can learn from each other such, often highly abstract, rules of conduct by example and imitation (or 'by analogy'), although neither those who set the examples nor those who learn from them may be consciously aware of the existence of the rules which they nevertheless strictly observe. This is a problem most familiar to us in the learning of language by children who are able to produce correctly most complicated expressions they have never heard before;[17] but it occurs also in such fields as manners, morals and law, and in most skills where we are guided by rules which we know how to follow but are unable to state.

The important point is that every man growing up in a given culture will find in himself rules, or may discover that he acts in accordance with rules—and will similarly recognize the actions of others as conforming or not conforming to various rules. This is, of course, not proof that they are a permanent or unalterable part of 'human nature', or that they are innate, but proof only that they are part of a cultural heritage which is likely to be fairly constant, especially so long as they are not articulated in words and therefore also are not discussed or consciously examined.

The false dichotomy of 'natural' and 'artificial'

The discussion of the problems with which we are concerned was long hampered by the universal acceptance of a misleading distinction which was introduced by the ancient Greeks and from whose confusing effect we have not yet wholly freed ourselves. This is the division of phenomena between those which in modern terms are 'natural' and those which are 'artificial'. The original Greek terms, which seem to have been introduced by the Sophists of the fifth century B.C., were *physei*, which means 'by nature' and, in contrast to it, either *nomō*, best rendered as 'by convention', or *thesei*, which means roughly 'by deliberate decision'.[18] The use of two terms with somewhat different meanings to express the second part of the division indicates the confusion which has beset the discussion ever since. The distinction intended may be either between objects which existed independently and objects which were the results of human *action*, or between objects which arose independently of, and objects which arose as the result of, human *design*. The failure to distinguish between these two meanings led to the situation where one author could argue with regard to a given phenomenon that it was artificial because it was the result of human action, while another might describe the same phenomenon as natural because it was evidently not the result of human design. Not until the eighteenth century did thinkers like Bernard Mandeville and David Hume make it clear that there existed a category of phenomena which, depending on which of the two definitions one adhered to, would fall into either the one or the other of the two categories and therefore ought to be assigned to a distinct third class of phenomena, later described by Adam Ferguson as 'the result of human action but not of human design'.[19] These were the phenomena which required for their explanation a distinct body of theory and which came to provide the object of the theoretical social sciences.

But in the more than two thousand years during which the distinction introduced by the ancient Greeks has ruled thought almost unchallenged, it has become deeply engrained in concepts and language. In the second century A.D. a Latin grammarian, Aulus Gellius, rendered the Greek terms *physei* and *thesei* by *naturalis* and *positivus*, from which most European languages derived the words to describe two kinds of law.[20]

There occurred later one promising development in the discussion of these questions by the medieval schoolmen, which led close to a recognition of the intermediate category of phenomena that were 'the result of human action but not of human design'. In the twelfth century some of those writers had begun to include under *naturalis* all that was not the result of human invention or a deliberate creation; [21] and in the course of time it came to be increasingly recognized that many social phenomena fell into this category. Indeed, in the discussion of the problems of society by the last of the schoolmen, the Spanish Jesuits of the sixteenth century, *naturalis* became a technical term for such social phenomena as were not deliberately shaped by human will. In the work of one of them, Luis Molina, it is, for example, explained that the 'natural price' is so called because 'it results from the thing itself without regard to laws and decrees, but is dependent on many circumstances which alter it, such as the sentiments of men, their estimation of different uses, often even in consequence of whims and pleasures'. [22] Indeed, these ancestors of ours thought and 'acted under a strong impression of the ignorance and fallibility of mankind', [23] and, for instance, argued that the precise 'mathematical price' at which a commodity could be justly sold was only known to God, because it depended on more circumstances than any man could know, and that therefore the determination of the 'just price' must be left to the market. [24]

These beginnings of an evolutionary approach were submerged, however, in the sixteenth and seventeenth centuries by the rise of constructivist rationalism, with the result that both the term 'reason' and the term 'natural law' completely changed their meaning. 'Reason', which had included the capacity of the mind to distinguish between good and evil, that is between what was and what was not in accordance with established rules, [25] came to mean a capacity to construct such rules by deduction from explicit premises. The conception of natural law was thereby turned into that of a 'law of reason' and thus almost into the opposite of what it had meant. This new rationalist law of nature of Grotius and his successors, [26] indeed, shared with its positivist antagonists the conception that all law was made by reason or could at least be fully justified by it, and differed from it only in the assumption that law could be logically derived from *a priori* premises, while positivism regarded it as a deliberate construction based on empirical knowledge of the effects it would have on the achievement of desirable human purposes.

The rise of the evolutionary approach

After the Cartesian relapse into anthropomorphic thinking on these matters a new start was made by Bernard Mandeville and David Hume. They were probably inspired more by the tradition of the English common law, especially as expounded by Matthew Hale, than by the the law of nature. [27] It came increasingly to be seen that the formation of regular patterns in human relations that were not the conscious aim of human actions raised a problem which required the development of a systematic social theory. This need was met during the second half of the eighteenth century in the field of economics by the Scottish moral philosophers, led by Adam Smith and Adam Ferguson, while the consequences to be drawn for political theory received their magnificent formulations from the great seer Edmund Burke, in whose work we shall, however, seek in vain for a systematic theory. But while in England the development suffered a new setback from the intrusion of constructivism in the form of Benthamite utilitarianism, [28] it gained a new vitality on the continent from the 'historical schools' of linguistics and law. [29] After the beginnings made by the Scottish philosophers, the systematic development of the evolutionary aproach to social phenomena took place mainly in Germany through Wilhelm von Humboldt and F. C. von Savigny. We cannot consider here that development in linguistics, although for a long time it was the only field outside of economics where a coherent theory was achieved, and the extent to which since Roman times the theory of law has been fertilized by conceptions borrowed from the grammarians deserves to be better understood than it is. [30] In the social sciences it was through Savigny's follower Sir Henry Maine [31] that the evolutionary approach re-entered the English tradition. And in the great survey of 1883 of the methods of the social sciences by the founder of the Austrian school of economics, Carl Menger, the central position for all social sciences of the problem of the spontaneous formation of institutions and its genetic character was most fully restated on the continent. In recent times the tradition has been most fruitfully developed by cultural anthropology, at least some of whose leading figures are fully aware of this ancestry. [32]

As the conception of evolution will play a central role throughout our discussion, it is important to clear up some misunderstandings which in recent times have made students of society reluctant to employ it. The first is the erroneous belief that it is a conception which the social sciences have borrowed from biology. It was in fact the other way round, and if Charles Darwin was able successfully to apply to biology a concept which he had largely learned from the social sciences, this does not make it less important in the field in which it originated. It was in the discussion of such social formations as language and morals, law and money, that in the eighteenth century the twin conceptions of evolution and the spontaneous formation of an order were at last clearly formulated, and provided the intellectual tools which Darwin and his contemporaries were able to apply to biological evolution. Those eighteenth-century moral philosophers and the historical schools of law and language might well be described, as some of the theorists of language of the nineteenth century indeed described themselves, as Darwinians before Darwin. [33]

A nineteenth-century social theorist who needed Darwin to teach him the idea of evolution was not worth his salt. Unfortunately some did, and produced views which under the name of 'Social Darwinism' have since been responsible for the distrust with which the concept of evolution has been regarded by social scientists. There are, of course, important differences between the manner in which the process of selection operates in the cultural transmission that leads to the formation of social institutions, and the manner in which it operates in the selection of innate biological characteristics and their transmission by physiological inheritance. The error of 'Social Darwinism' was that it concentrated on the selection of individuals rather than on that of institutions and practices, and on the selection of innate rather than on culturally transmitted capacities of the individuals. But although the scheme of Darwinian theory has only limited application to the latter and its literal use leads to grave distortions, the basic conception of evolution is still the same in both fields.

The other great misunderstanding which has led to a discrediting of the theory of social evolution, is the belief that the theory of evolution consists of 'laws of evolution'. This is true at most in a special sense of the word 'law', and is certainly not true, as it is often thought, in the sense of a statement of a necessary sequence of particular stages or phases through which the process of evolution must pass and which by extrapolation leads to predictions of the future course of evolution. The theory of evolution proper provides no more than an account of a process the outcome of which will depend on a very large number of particular facts, far too numerous for us to know in their entirety, and therefore does not lead to predictions about the future. We are in consequence confined to 'explanations of the principle' or to predictions merely of the abstract pattern the process will follow.[34]

The pretended laws of overall evolution supposedly derived from observation have in fact nothing to do with the legitimate theory of evolution which accounts for the process. They derive from the altogether different conceptions of the historicism of Comte, Hegel and Marx, and their holistic approach, and assert a purely mystical necessity that evolution must run a certain predetermined course. Although it must be admitted that the original meaning of the term 'evolution' refers to such an 'unwinding' of potentialities already contained in the germ, the process by which the biological and social theory of evolution accounts for the appearence of different complex structures does not imply such a succession of particular steps. Those to whom the concept of evolution implies necessary sequences of predetermined 'stages', or 'phrases', through which the development of an organism or a social institution must pass, are therefore justified in rejecting such a conception of evolution, for which there is no scientific warrant.

We will mention at this point only briefly that the frequent attempts made to use the conception of evolution, not merely as an explanation of the rise of rules of conduct, but as the basis of a prescriptive science of ethics, also have no foundation in the legitimate theory of evolution, but belong to those extrapolations of observed tendencies as 'laws of evolution' for which there is no justification. This needs saying here as some distinguished biologists who certainly understand the theory of evolution proper have been tempted into such assertions.[35] It is our concern here, however, only to show that such abuses of the concept of evolution in subjects like anthropology, ethics, and also law, which have discredited it for a time, were based on a misconception of the nature of the theory of evolution; and that, if it is taken in its correct meaning, it still remains true that the complex, spontaneously formed structures with which social theory has to deal, can be understood only as the result of a process of evolution and that, therefore, here 'the genetic element is inseparable from the idea of theoretical sciences'.[36]

The persistence of constructivism in current thought

It is difficult to appreciate fully the extent to which the constructivist fallacy has during the last three hundred years determined the attitudes of many of the most independent and courageous thinkers. The rejection of the accounts which religion gave of the source and grounds of validity of the traditional rules of morals and law led to the rejection of these rules themselves so far as they could not be rationally justified. It was to their achievement in thus 'freeing' the human mind that many of the celebrated thinkers of the period owe their fame. We can here illustrate this only by picking out almost at random a few characteristic instances. [37]

One of the best known is, of course, Voltaire, whose views on the problem with which we shall be mainly concerned found expression in the exhortation, 'if you want good laws, burn those you have and make new ones'. [38] Even greater influence was exercised by Rousseau; of him it has been well said that: [39]

> There was even no law except law willed by living men—this
> was his greatest heresy from many points of view, including
> the Christian; it was also his greatest affirmation in political
> theory. . . . What he did, and it was revolutionary enough, was
> to undermine the faith of many people in the justice of the
> society in which they lived.

And he did so by demanding that 'society' should be just as if it were a thinking being.

The refusal to recognize as binding any rules of conduct whose justification had not been rationally demonstrated or 'made clear and demonstrative to every individual' [40] becomes in the nineteenth century an ever recurring theme. Two examples will indicate the attitude. Early in that century we find Alexander Herzen arguing: 'You want a book of rules, while I think that when one reaches a certain age one ought to be ashamed of having to use one [because] the truly free man creates his own morality.' [41] And quite in the same manner a distinguished contemporary positivist philosopher contends that 'the power of reason must be sought not in rules that reason dictates to our imagination, but in the ability to free ourselves from any kind of rules to which we have been conditioned through experience and traditions'. [42]

The best description of this state of mind by a representative thinker of our time is found in the account given by Lord Keynes in a talk entitled 'My early beliefs'. [43] Speaking in 1938 about the time thirty-five years before, when he himself was twenty, he says of himself and his friends:

We entirely repudiated a personal liability on us to obey general rules. We claimed the right to judge every individual case on its merits, and the wisdom, experience, and self-control to do so successfully. This was a very important part of our faith, violently and aggressively held, and for the outer world it was our most obvious and dangerous characteristic. We repudiated entirely customary morals, conventions, and traditional wisdom. We were, that is to say, in the strict sense of the term, immoralists . . . we recognized no moral obligation, no inner sanction, to conform or obey. Before heaven we claimed to be our own judge in our own case.

To which he added: 'So far as I am concerned, it is too late to change. I remain, and always will remain, an immoralist.'

To anyone who has himself grown up before the First World War, it is obvious that this was then not an attitude peculiar to the Bloomsbury Group, but a very widespread one, shared by many of the most active and independent spirits of the time.

Our anthropomorphic language

How deeply the erroneous constructivist or intentionalist interpretation pervades our thinking about the phenomena of society is seen when we consider the meaning of many of the terms which we have to use in referring to them. Indeed, most of the errors against which we shall have to argue throughout this book are so deeply built into our language that the use of established terms will lead the unwary almost necessarily to wrong conclusions. The language which we have to use has developed in the course of millennia when man could conceive of an order only as the product of design, and when he regarded as evidence of the action of a personal designer whatever order he discovered in the phenomena. In consequence, practically all the terms that are available to us to describe such orderly structures or their functioning are charged with the suggestion that a personal agent has created them. Because of this they regularly lead to false conclusions.

To some extent this is true of all scientific vocabulary. The physical sciences no less than biology or social theory had to make use of terms of anthropomorphic origin. But the physicist who speaks of 'force' or 'inertia' or of a body 'acting' on another employs these terms in a generally understood technical sense not likely to mislead. But to speak of society as 'acting' at once conjures up associations which are very misleading.

We shall in general refer to this propensity as 'anthropomorphism', although the term is not wholly accurate. To be more exact we ought to distinguish between the even more primitive attitude which *personifies* such entities as society by ascribing to them possession of a mind and which is properly described as *anthropomorphism* or *animism*, and the slightly more sophisticated interpretation which ascribes their order and functioning to the *design* of some distinct agency, and which is better described as *intentionalism, artificialism*,[44] or, as we do here, *constructivism*. However, these two propensities shade into each other more or less imperceptibly, and for our purposes we shall generally use 'anthropomorphism' without making the finer distinction.

Since practically the whole vocabulary available for the discussion of the spontaneous orders with which we shall be concerned possesses such misleading connotations, we must in some degree be arbitrary in deciding which words we shall use in a strictly non-anthropomorphic sense and which we shall use only if we want to imply intention or design. To preserve clarity, however, it is essential that with respect to many words we use them either for the results of deliberate constructions only, or for the results of spontaneous formation only, but not for both. Sometimes, however, as in the case of the term 'order', it will be necessary to use it in a neutral sense comprising both spontaneous orders and 'organizations' or 'arrangements'. The last two terms, which we shall use only for results of design, illustrate the fact that it is often as difficult to find terms which always imply design as it is to find those which do not suggest it. The biologist will generally without hesitation speak of 'organization' without implying design, but it would sound odd if he said that an organism not only had but was an organization or that it had been organized. The role that the term 'organization' has played in the development of modern political thought, and the meaning which modern 'organization theory' attaches to it, seem to justify in the present context a restriction of its meaning to results of design only.

Since the distinction between a made order and one which forms itself as a result of regularities of the actions of its elements will be the chief topic of the next chapter, we need not dwell upon it here any further. And in volume 2 we shall have to consider at some length the almost invariably confusing character of the little word 'social' which, because of its particularly elusive character, carries confusion into almost any statement in which it is used.

We shall find too that such current notions as that society 'acts' or that it 'treats', 'rewards', or 'remunerates' persons, or that it 'values' or 'owns' or 'controls' objects or services, or is 'responsible for' or 'guilty of' something, or that it has a 'will' or 'purpose', can be 'just' or 'unjust', or that the economy 'distributes' or 'allocates' resources, all suggest a false intentionalist or constructivist interpretation of words which might have been used without such a connotation, but which almost inevitably lead the user to illegitimate conclusions. We shall see that such confusions are at the root of the basic conceptions of highly influential schools of thought which have wholly succumbed to the belief that all rules or laws must have been invented or explicitly agreed upon by somebody. Only when it is wrongly assumed that all rules of just conduct have deliberately been made by somebody do such sophisms become plausible as that all power of making laws must be arbitrary, or that there must always exist an ultimate 'sovereign' source of power from which all law derives. Many of the age-old puzzles of political theory and many of the conceptions which have profoundly affected the evolution of political institutions are the product of this confusion. This is especially true of that tradition in legal theory which more than any other is proud of having fully escaped from anthropomorphic conceptions, namely legal positivism; for it proves on examination to be entirely based on what we have called the constructivist fallacy. It is actually one of the main offshoots of that rationalist constructivism which, in taking literally the expression that man has 'made' all his culture and institutions, has been driven to the fiction that all law is the product of somebody's will.

One more term whose ambiguity had a similar confusing effect on social theory, and particularly on some positivist theories of law, and which therefore ought to be briefly mentioned here, is the term 'function'. It is an almost indispensable term for the discussion of those self-maintaining structures which we find alike in biological organisms and in spontaneous social orders. Such a function may be performed without the acting part knowing what purpose its action serves. But the characteristic anthropomorphism of the positivist tradition has led to a curious perversion: from the discovery that an institution served a function the conclusion was drawn that the persons performing the function must be directed to do so by another human will. Thus the true insight that the institution of private property served a function necessary for the maintenance of the spontaneous order of society led to the belief that for this purpose a power of direction of some authority was required—an opinion even expressly laid down in the constitutions of some countries which were drawn up under positivist inspiration.

Reason and abstraction

The aspects of the Cartesian tradition which we have described as constructivism are often also referred to simply as rationalism, and this is apt to give rise to a misunderstanding. It has, for instance, become customary to speak of its early critics, especially Bernard Mandeville and David Hume, as 'anti-rationalists'[45] and this has conveyed the impression that these 'anti-rationalists' were less concerned to achieve the most effective use of reason than those who specially claimed the name of rationalists. The fact is, however, that the so-called anti-rationalists insist that to make reason as effective as possible requires an insight into the limitations of the powers of conscious reason and into the assistance we obtain from processes of which we are not aware, an insight which constructivist rationalism lacks. Thus, if the desire to make reason as effective as possible is what is meant by rationalism, I am myself a rationalist. If, however, the term means that conscious reason ought to determine every particular action, I am not a rationalist, and such rationalism seems to me to be very unreasonable. Surely, one of the tasks of reason is to decide how far it is to extend its control or how far it ought to rely on other forces which it cannot wholly control. It is therefore better in this connection not to distinguish between 'rationalism' and 'anti-rationalism' but to distinguish between a constructivist and an evolutionary, or, in Karl Popper's terms, a naïve and a critical rationalism.

Connected with the uncertain meaning of the term 'rationalism' are the opinions generally held about the attitude to 'abstraction' characteristic of 'rationalism'. The name is often even used to describe an undue addiction to abstraction. The characteristic property of constructivist rationalism, however, is rather that it is not content with abstraction—that it does not recognize that abstract concepts are a means to cope with the complexity of the concrete which our mind is not capable of fully mastering. Evolutionary rationalism, on the other hand, recognizes abstractions as the indispensable means of the mind which enable it to deal with a reality it cannot fully comprehend. This is connected with the fact that in the constructivist view 'abstractness' is conceived as a property confined to conscious thought or concepts, while actually it is a characteristic possessed by all the processes which determine action long before they appear in conscious thought or are expressed in language. Whenever a *type* of situation evokes in an individual a *disposition* towards a certain *pattern* of response, that basic relation which is described as 'abstract' is present. There can be little doubt that the peculiar capacities of a central nervous system consist precisely in the fact that particular stimuli do not directly evoke particular responses, but make it possible for certain classes or configurations of stimuli to set up certain dispositions towards classes of actions, and that only the superimposition of many such dispositions specify the particular action that will result. This 'primacy of the abstract', as I have called it elsewhere, [46] will be assumed throughout this book.

Abstractness will here be regarded, therefore, not only as a property possessed to a greater or lesser degree by all (conscious or unconscious) mental processes, but as the basis of man's capacity to move successfully in a world very imperfectly known to him— an adaptation to his ignorance of most of the particular facts of his surroundings. The main purpose of our stress on the rules which govern our actions is to bring out the central importance of the abstract character of all mental processes.

Thus considered, abstraction is not something which the mind produces by processes of logic from its perception of reality, but rather a property of the categories with which it operates—not a product of the mind but rather what constitutes the mind. We never act, and could never act, in full consideration of all the facts of a particular situation, but always by singling out as relevant only some aspects of it; not by conscious choice or deliberate selection, but by a mechanism over which we do not exercise deliberate control.

It will perhaps be clear now that our constant stress on the non-rational character of much of our actions is meant not to belittle or criticize this manner of acting, but, on the contrary, to bring out one of the reasons why it is successful; and not to suggest that we ought to try fully to understand why we do what we do, but to point out that this is impossible; and that we can make use of so much experience, not because we possess that experience, but because, without our knowing it, it has become incorporated in the schemata of thought which guide us.

There are two possible misconceptions of the position taken which we must try to prevent. One derives from the fact that action which is guided by rules we are not aware of is often described as 'instinctive' or 'intuitive'. There is not much harm in these words except that both, and specially 'intuitive', usually refer to the perception of the particular and relatively concrete, while what we are here concerned with are capacities determining very general or abstract properties of the actions taken. As commonly used, the term 'intuitive' suggests an attribute not possessed by abstract rules which we follow in our actions, and for this reason it had better be avoided.

The other possible misunderstanding of our position is the impression that the emphasis we place on the non-conscious character of many of the rules which govern our action is connected with the conception of an unconscious or subconscious mind underlying the theories of psychoanalysis or 'depth-psychology'. But although to some extent the two views may aim at an explanation of the same phenomena, they are in fact wholly different. We shall not use, and in fact regard as unwarranted and false, the whole conception of an unconscious mind which differs from the conscious mind only by being unconscious, but in all other respects operates in the same, rational, goal-seeking manner as the conscious mind. Nothing is gained by postulating such a mystical entity, or by ascribing to the various propensities or rules which together produce the complex order we call mind any of the properties which the resulting order possesses. Psychoanalysis seems in this respect merely to have created another ghost which in turn is held to govern the 'ghost in the machine' [47] of Cartesian dualism.

Why the extreme forms of constructivist rationalism regularly lead to a revolt against reason

In conclusion of this introductory chapter some observations are in place on a phenomenon which transcends the scope of this book but which is of considerable importance for the understanding of its immediate concerns. We refer to the fact that the constructivist rationalism which knows no bounds to the applications of conscious reason has historically again and again given birth to a revolt against reason. Indeed, this development, in which an over-estimation of the powers of reason leads through disillusionment to a violent reaction against the guidance by abstract reason, and to an extolling of the powers of the particular will, is not in the least paradoxical, but almost inevitable.

The illusion that leads constructivist rationalists regularly to an enthronement of the will consists in the belief that reason can transcend the realm of the abstract and by itself is able to determine the desirability of particular actions. Yet it is always only in combination with particular, non-rational impulses that reason can determine what to do, and its function is essentially to act as a restraint on emotion, or to steer action impelled by other factors. The illusion that reason alone can tell us what we ought to do, and that therefore all reasonable men ought to be able to join in the endeavour to pursue common ends as members of an organization, is quickly dispelled when we attempt to put it into practice. But the desire to use our reason to turn the whole of society into one rationally directed engine persists, and in order to realize it common ends are imposed upon all that cannot be justified by reason and cannot be more than the decisions of particular wills.

The rationalist revolt against reason, if we may so call it, is usually directed against the abstractness of thought. It will not recognize that all thought must remain abstract to various degrees and that therefore it can never by itself fully determine particular actions. Reason is merely a discipline, an insight into the limitations of the possibilities of successful action, which often will tell us only what not to do. This discipline is necessary precisely because our intellect is not capable of grasping reality in all its complexity. Although the use of abstraction extends the scope of phenomena which we can master intellectually, it does so by limiting the degree to which we can foresee the effects of our actions, and therefore also by limiting to certain general features the degree to which we can shape the world to our liking. Liberalism for this reason restricts deliberate control of the overall order of society to the enforcement of such general rules as are necessary for the formation of a spontaneous order, the details of which we cannot foresee.

Perhaps nobody has seen this connection between liberalism and the insight into the limited powers of abstract thinking more clearly than that ultra-rationalist who has become the fountain head of most modern irrationalism and totalitarianism, G. W. F. Hegel. When he wrote that 'the view which clings to abstraction is *liberalism,* over which the concrete always prevails and which always founders in the struggle against it', [48] he truly described the fact that we are not yet mature enough to submit for any length of time to strict discipline of reason and allow our emotions constantly to break through its restraints.

The reliance on the abstract is thus not a result of an over-estimation but rather of an insight into the limited powers of our reason. It is the over-estimation of the powers of reason which leads to the revolt against the submission to abstract rules. Constructivist rationalism rejects the demand for this discipline of reason because it deceives itself that reason can directly master all the particulars; and it is thereby led to a preference for the concrete over the abstract, the particular over the general, because its adherents do not realize how much they thereby limit the span of true control by reason. The *hubris* of reason manifests itself in those who believe that they can dispense with abstraction and achieve a full mastery of the concrete and thus positively master the social process. The desire to remodel society after the image of individual man, which since Hobbes has governed rationalist political theory, and which attributes to the Great Society properties which only individuals or deliberately created organizations can possess, leads to a striving not merely to be, but to make everything rational. Although we must endeavour to make society good in the sense that we shall like to live in it, we cannot make it good in the sense that it will behave morally. It does not make sense to apply the standards of conscious conduct to those unintended consequences of individual action which all the truly social represents, except by eliminating the unintended—which would mean eliminating all that we call culture.

The Great Society and the civilization it has made possible is the product of man's growing capacity to communicate abstract thought; and when we say that what all men have in common is their reason we mean their common capacity for abstract thought. That man uses this capacity largely without explicitly knowing the abstract principles which guide him, and does not understand all the reasons for allowing himself to be thus guided, has produced a situation in which the very over-estimation of those powers of reason of which man is conscious has led him to hold in contempt what has made reason as powerful as it is: its abstract character. It was the failure to recognize that abstractions help our reason go further than it could if it tried to master all the particulars which produced a host of schools of philosophy inimical to abstract reason —philosophies of the concrete, of 'life' and of 'existence' which extol emotion, the particular and the instinctive, and which are only too ready to support such emotions as those of race, nation, and class.

Thus constructivist rationalism, in its endeavour to make everything subject to rational control, in its preference for the concrete and its refusal to submit to the discipline of abstract rules, comes to join hands with irrationalism. Construction is possible only in the service of particular ends which in the last resort must be non-rational, and on which no rational argument can produce agreement if it is not already present at the outset.

TWO

COSMOS AND TAXIS

The man of system . . . seems to imagine that he can arrange
the different members of a great society with as much ease
as the hand arranges the different pieces upon a chessboard.
He does not consider that the pieces upon the chessboard have
no other principle of motion besides that which the hand
impresses upon them; but that, in the great chessboard of human
society, every single piece has a principle of motion of its own,
altogether different from that which the legislature might choose
to impress upon it. If those two principles coincide and act in the
same direction, the game of human society will go on easily and
harmoniously, and is very likely to be happy and successful. If
they are opposite or different, the game will go on miserably and
the society must be at all times in the highest degree of disorder.

Adam Smith*

The concept of order

The central concept around which the discussion of this book will
turn is that of order, and particularly the distinction between two
kinds of order which we will provisionally call 'made' and 'grown'
orders. Order is an indispensable concept for the discussion of all
complex phenomena, in which it must largely play the role the
concept of law plays in the analysis of simpler phenomena.[1] There
is no adequate term other than 'order' by which we can describe it,
although 'system', 'structure' or 'pattern' may occasionally serve
instead. The term 'order' has, of course, a long history in the social
sciences,[2] but in recent times it has generally been avoided, largely
because of the ambiguity of its meaning and its frequent association
with authoritarian views. We cannot do without it, however, and
shall have to guard against misinterpretation by sharply defining
the general sense in which we shall employ it and then clearly
distinguishing between the two different ways in which such order
can originate.

By 'order' we shall thoughout describe *a state of affairs in which a multiplicity of elements of various kinds are so related to each other that we may learn from our acquaintance with some spatial or temporal part of the whole to form correct expectations concerning the rest, or at least expectations which have a good chance of proving correct.* [3] It is clear that every society must in this sense possess an order and that such an order will often exist without having been deliberately created. As has been said by a distinguished social anthropologist, 'that there is some order, consistency and constancy in social life, is obvious. If there were not, none of us would be able to go about our affairs or satisfy our most elementary needs.' [4]

Living as members of society and dependent for the satisfaction of most of our needs on various forms of co-operation with others, we depend for the effective pursuit of our aims clearly on the correspondence of the expectations concerning the actions of others on which our plans are based with what they will really do. This matching of the intentions and expectations that determine the actions of different individuals is the form in which order manifests itself in social life; and it will be the question of how such an order does come about that will be our immediate concern. The first answer to which our anthropomorphic habits of thought almost inevitably lead us is that it must be due to the design of some thinking mind. [5] And because order has been generally interpreted as such a deliberate *arrangement* by somebody, the concept has become unpopular among most friends of liberty and has been favoured mainly by authoritarians. According to this interpretation order in society must rest on a relation of command and obedience, or a hierarchical structure of the whole of society in which the will of superiors, and ultimately of some single supreme authority, determines what each individual must do.

This authoritarian connotation of the concept of order derives, however, entirely from the belief that order can be created only by forces outside the system (or 'exogenously'). It does not apply to an equilibrium set up from within [6] (or 'endogenously') such as that which the general theory of the market endeavours to explain. A spontaneous order of this kind has in many respects properties different from those of a made order.

The two sources of order

The study of spontaneous orders has long been the peculiar task of economic theory, although, of course, biology has from its beginning been concerned with that special kind of spontaneous order which we call an organism. Only recently has there arisen within the physical sciences under the name of cybernetics a special discipline which is also concerned with what are called self-organizing or self-generating systems. [7]

The distinction of this kind of order from one which has been made by somebody putting the elements of a set in their places or directing their movements is indispensable for any understanding of the processes of society as well as for all social policy. There are several terms available for describing each kind of order. The made order which we have already referred to as an exogenous order or an arrangement may again be described as a construction, an artificial order or, especially where we have to deal with a directed social order, as an *organization*. The grown order, on the other hand, which we have referred to as a self-generating or endogenous order, is in English most conveniently described as a *spontaneous order*. Classical Greek was more fortunate in possessing distinct single words for the two kinds of order, namely *taxis* for a made order, such as, for example, an order of battle, [8] and *kosmos* for a grown order, meaning originally 'a right order in a state or a community'. [9] We shall occasionally avail ourselves of these Greek words as technical terms to describe the two kinds of order.

It would be no exaggeration to say that social theory begins with—and has an object only because of—the discovery that there exist orderly structures which are the product of the action of many men but are not the result of human design. In some fields this is now universally accepted. Although there was a time when men believed that even language and morals had been 'invented' by some genius of the past, everybody recognizes now that they are the outcome of a process of evolution whose results nobody foresaw or designed. But in other fields many people still treat with suspicion the claim that the patterns of interaction of many men can show an order that is of nobody's deliberate making; in the economic sphere, in particular, critics still pour uncomprehending ridicule on Adam Smith's expression of the 'invisible hand' by which, in the language of his time, he described how man is led 'to promote an end which was no part of his intentions'. [10] If indignant reformers still complain of the chaos of economic affairs, insinuating a complete absence of order, this is partly because they cannot conceive of an order which is not deliberately made, and partly because to them an order means something aiming at concrete purposes which is, as we shall see, what a spontaneous order cannot do.

We shall examine later (see volume 2, chapter 10) how that coincidence of expectations and plans is produced which characterizes the market order and the nature of the benefits we derive from it. For the moment we are concerned only with the fact that an order not made by man does exist and with the reasons why this is not more readily recognized. The main reason is that such orders as that of the market do not obtrude themselves on our senses but have to be traced by our intellect. We cannot see, or otherwise intuitively perceive, this order of meaningful actions, but are only able mentally to reconstruct it by tracing the relations that exist between the elements. We shall describe this feature by saying that it is an abstract and not a concrete order.

The distinguishing properties of spontaneous orders

One effect of our habitually identifying order with a made order or *taxis* is indeed that we tend to ascribe to all order certain properties which deliberate arrangements regularly, and with respect to some of these properties necessarily, possess. Such orders are relatively *simple* or at least necessarily confined to such moderate degrees of complexity as the maker can still survey; they are usually *concrete* in the sense just mentioned that their existence can be intuitively perceived by inspection; and, finally, having been made deliberately, they invariably do (or at one time did) *serve a purpose* of the maker. None of these characteristics necessarily belong to a spontaneous order or *kosmos*. Its degree of complexity is not limited to what a human mind can master. Its existence need not manifest itself to our senses but may be based on purely *abstract* relations which we can only mentally reconstruct. And not having been made it *cannot* legitimately be said to *have a particular purpose*, although our awareness of its existence may be extremely important for our successful pursuit of a great variety of different purposes.

Spontaneous orders are not necessarily complex, but unlike deliberate human arrangements, they may achieve any degree of complexity. One of our main contentions will be that very complex orders, comprising more particular facts than any brain could ascertain or manipulate, can be brought about only through forces inducing the formation of spontaneous orders.

Spontaneous orders need not be what we have called abstract, but they will often consist of a system of abstract relations between elements which are also defined only by abstract properties, and for this reason will not be intuitively perceivable and not recognizable except on the basis of a theory accounting for their character. The significance of the abstract character of such orders rests on the fact that they may persist while all the particular elements they comprise, and even the number of such elements, change. All that is necessary to preserve such an abstract order is that a certain structure of relationships be maintained, or that elements of a certain kind (but variable in number) continue to be related in a certain manner.

Most important, however, is the relation of a spontaneous order to the conception of purpose. Since such an order has not been created by an outside agency, the order as such also can have no purpose, although its existence may be very serviceable to the individuals which move within such order. But in a different sense it may well be said that the order rests on purposive action of its elements, when 'purpose' would, of course, mean nothing more than that their actions tend to secure the preservation or restoration of that order. The use of 'purposive' in this sense as a sort of 'teleological shorthand', as it has been called by biologists, is unobjectionable so long as we do not imply an awareness of purpose of the part of the elements, but mean merely that the elements have acquired regularities of conduct conducive to the maintenance of the order—presumably because those who did act in certain ways had within the resulting order a better chance of survival than those who did not. In general, however, it is preferable to avoid in this connection the term 'purpose' and to speak instead of 'function'.

Spontaneous orders in nature

It will be instructive to consider briefly the character of some spontaneous orders which we find in nature, since here some of their characteristic properties stand out most clearly. There are in the physical world many instances of complex orders which we could bring about only by availing ourselves of the known forces which tend to lead to their formation, and never by deliberately placing each element in the appropriate position. We can never produce a crystal or a complex organic compound by placing the individual atoms in such a position that they will form the lattice of a crystal or the system based on benzol rings which make up an organic compound. But we can create the conditions in which they will arrange themselves in such a manner.

What does in these instances determine not only the general character of the crystal or compound that will be formed but also the particular position of any one element in them? The important point is that the regularity of the conduct of the elements will determine the general character of the resulting order but not all the detail of its particular manifestation. The particular manner in which the resulting abstract order will manifest itself will depend, in addition to the rules which govern the actions of the elements, on their initial position and on all the particular circumstances of the immediate environment to which each of them will react in the course of the formation of that order. The order, in other words, will always be an adaptation to a large number of particular facts which will not be known in their totality to anyone.

We should note that a regular pattern will thus form itself not only if the elements all obey the same rules and their different actions are determined only by the different positions of the several individuals relatively to each other, but also, as is true in the case of the chemical compound, if there are different kinds of elements which act in part according to different rules. Whichever is the case, we shall be able to predict only the general character of the order that will form itself, and not the particular position which any particular element will occupy relatively to any other element.

Another example from physics is in some respects even more instructive. In the familiar school experiment in which iron filings on a sheet of paper are made to arrange themselves along some of the lines of force of a magnet placed below, we can predict the general shape of the chains that will be formed by the filings hooking themselves together; but we cannot predict along which ones of the family of an infinite number of such curves that define the magnetic field these chains will place themselves. This will depend on the position, direction, weight, roughness or smoothness of each of the iron filings and on all the irregularities of the surface of the paper. The forces emanating from the magnet and from each of the iron filings will thus interact with the environment to produce a unique instance of a general pattern, the general character of which will be determined by known laws, but the concrete appearance of which will depend on particular circumstances we cannot fully ascertain.

*In society, reliance on spontaneous order both extends and
limits our powers of control*

Since a spontaneous order results from the individual elements
adapting themselves to circumstances which directly affect only
some of them, and which in their totality need not be known to
anyone, it may extend to circumstances so complex that no mind
can comprehend them all. Consequently, the concept becomes particularly important when we turn from mechanical to such 'more
highly organized' or essentially complex phenomena as we encounter in the realms of life, mind and society. Here we have to deal with
'grown' structures with a degree of complexity which they have
assumed and could assume only because they were produced by
spontaneous ordering forces. They in consequence present us
with peculiar difficulties in our effort to explain them as well as in
any attempt to influence their character. Since we can know at most
the rules observed by the elements of various kinds of which the
structures are made up, but not all the individual elements and
never all the particular circumstances in which each of them is
placed, our knowledge will be restricted to the general character of
the order which will form itself. And even where, as is true of a
society of human beings, we may be in a position to alter at least
some of the rules of conduct which the elements obey, we shall
thereby be able to influence only the general character and not the
detail of the resulting order.

This means that, though the use of spontaneous ordering forces
enables us to induce the formation of an order of such a degree of
complexity (namely comprising elements of such numbers, di-
versity and variety of conditions) as we could never master intellectually, or deliberately arrange, we will have less power over the details of such an order than we would of one which we produce by
arrangement. In the case of spontaenous orders we may, by determining some of the factors which shape them, determine their
abstract features, but we will have to leave the particulars to circumstances which we do not know. Thus, by relying on the spontaneously ordering forces, we can extend the scope or range of the
order which we may induce to form, precisely because its particular
manifestation will depend on many more circumstances than can
be known to us—and in the case of a social order, because such an
order will utilize the separate knowledge of all its several members, without this knowledge ever being concentrated in a single

mind, or being subject to those processes of deliberate coordination and adaptation which a mind performs.

In consequence, the degree of power of control over the extended and more complex order will be much smaller than that which we could exercise over a made order or *taxis*. There will be many aspects of it over which we will possess no control at all, or which at least we shall not be able to alter without interfering with—and to that extent impeding—the forces producing the spontaneous order. Any desire we may have concerning the particular position of individual elements, or the relation between particular individuals or groups, could not be satisfied without upsetting the overall order. The kind of power which in this respect we would possess over a concrete arrangement or *taxis* we would not have over a spontaneous order where we would know, and be able to influence, only the abstract aspects.

It is important to note here that there are two different respects in which order may be a matter of degree. How well ordered a set of objects or events is depends on how many of the attributes of (or the relations between) the elements we can learn to predict. Different orders may in this respect differ from each other in either or both of two ways: the orderliness may concern only very few relations between the elements, or a great many; and, second, the regularity thus defined may be great in the sense that it will be confirmed by all or nearly all instances, or it may be found to prevail only in a majority of the instances and thus allow us to predict its occurrence only with a certain degree of probability. In the first instance we may predict only a few of the features of the resulting structure, but do so with great confidence; such an order would be limited but may still be perfect. In the second instance we shall be able to predict much more, but with only a fair degree of certainty. The knowledge of the existence of an order will however still be useful even if this order is restricted in either or both these respects; and the reliance on spontaneously ordering forces may be preferable or even indispensable, although the order towards which a system tends will in fact be only more or less imperfectly approached. The market order in particular will regularly secure only a certain probability that the expected relations will prevail, but it is, nevertheless, the only way in which so many activities depending on dispersed knowledge can be effectively integrated into a single order.

Spontaneous orders result from their elements obeying certain rules of conduct

We have already indicated that the formation of spontaneous orders is the result of their elements following certain rules in their responses to their immediate environment. The nature of these rules still needs fuller examination, partly because the word 'rule' is apt to suggest some erroneous ideas, and partly because the rules which determine a spontaneous order differ in important respects from another kind of rules which are needed in regulating an organization or *taxis*.

On the first point, the instances of spontaneous orders which we have given from physics are instructive because they clearly show that the rules which govern the actions of the elements of such spontaneous orders need not be rules which are 'known' to these elements; it is sufficient that the elements actually behave in a manner which can be described by such rules. The concept of rules as we use it in this context therefore does not imply that such rules exist in articulated ('verbalized') forms, but only that it is possible to discover rules which the actions of the individuals in fact follow. To emphasize this we have occasionally spoken of 'regularity' rather than of rules, but regularity, of course, means simply that the elements behave according to rules.

That rules in this sense exist and operate without being explicitly known to those who obey them applies also to many of the rules which govern the actions of men and thereby determine a spontaneous social order. Man certainly does not know all the rules which guide his actions in the sense that he is able to state them in words. At least in primitive human society, scarcely less than in animal societies, the structure of social life is determined by rules of conduct which manifest themselves only by being in fact observed. Only when individual intellects begin to differ to a significant degree will it become necessary to express these rules in a form in which they can be communicated and explicitly taught, deviant behaviour corrected, and differences of opinion about appropriate behaviour decided. Although man never existed without laws that he obeyed, he did, of course, exist for hundreds of thousands of years without laws he 'knew' in the sense that he was able to articulate them.

What is of still greater importance in this connection, however, is that not every regularity in the behaviour of the elements does

43

secure an overall order. Some rules governing individual behaviour might clearly make altogether impossible the formation of an over-all order. Our problem is what kind of rules of conduct will produce an order of society and what kind of order particular rules will produce.

The classical instance of rules of the behaviour of the elements which will not produce order comes from the physical sciences: it is the second law of thermodynamics or the law of enthropy, according to which the tendency of the molecules of a gas to move at constant speeds in straight lines produces a state for which the term 'perfect disorder' has been coined. Similarly, it is evident that in society some perfectly regular behaviour of the individuals could produce only disorder: if the rule were that any individual should try to kill any other he encountered, or flee as soon as he saw another, the result would clearly be the complete impossibility of an order in which the activities of the individuals were based on collaboration with others.

Society can thus exist only if by a process of selection rules have evolved which lead individuals to behave in a manner which makes social life possible. It should be remembered that for this purpose selection will operate as between societies of different types, that is, be guided by the properties of their respective orders, but that the properties supporting this order will be properties of the individu-als, namely their propensity to obey certain rules of conduct on which the order of action of the group as a whole rests.

To put this differently: in a social order the particular circum-stances to which each individual will react will be those known to him. But the individual responses to particular circumstances will result in an overall order only if the individuals obey such rules as will produce an order. Even a very limited similarity in their be-haviour may be sufficient if the rules which they all obey are such as to produce an order. Such an order will always constitute an adaptation to the multitude of circumstances which are known to all the members of that society taken together but which are not known as a whole to any one person. This need not mean that the different persons will in similar circumstances do precisely the same thing; but merely that for the formation of such an overall order it is necessary that in some respects all individuals follow definite rules, or that their actions are limited to a certain range. In other words, the responses of the individuals to the events in their environment need be similar only in certain abstracts aspects to ensure that a determinate overall order will result.

44

The question which is of central importance as much for social theory as for social policy is thus what properties the rules must possess so that the separate actions of the individuals will produce an overall order. Some such rules all individuals of a society will obey because of the similar manner in which their environment represents itself to their minds. Other they will follow spontaneously because they will be part of their common cultural tradition. But there will be still others which they may have to be made to obey, since, although it would be in the interest of each to disregard them, the overall order on which the success of their actions depends will arise only if these rules are generally followed.

In a modern society based on exchange, one of the chief regularities in individual behaviour will result from the similarity of situations in which most individuals find themselves in working to earn an income; which means that they will normally prefer a larger return from their efforts to a smaller one, and often that they will increase their efforts in a particular direction if the prospects of return improve. This is a rule that will be followed at least with sufficient frequency to impress upon such a society an order of a certain kind. But the fact that most people will follow this rule will still leave the character of the resulting order very indeterminate, and by itself certainly would not be sufficient to give it a beneficial character. For the resulting order to be beneficial people must also observe some conventional rules, that is, rules which do not simply follow from their desires and their insight into relations of cause and effect, but which are normative and tell them what they ought to or ought not to do.

We shall later have to consider more fully the precise relation between the various kinds of rules which the people in fact obey and the resulting order of actions. Our main interest will then be those rules which, because we can deliberately alter them, become the chief instrument whereby we can affect the resulting order, namely the rules of law. At the moment our concern must be to make clear that while the rules on which a spontaneous order rests, may also be of spontaneous origin, this need not always be the case. Although undoubtedly an order originally formed itself spontaneously because the individuals followed rules which had not been deliberately made but had arisen spontaneously, people gradually learned to improve those rules; and it is at least conceivable that the formation of a spontaneous order relies entirely on rules that were deliberately made. The spontaneous character of the resulting order

45

must therefore be distinguished from the spontaneous origin of the rules on which it rests, and it is possible that an order which would still have to be described as spontaneous rests on rules which are entirely the result of deliberate design. In the kind of society with which we are familiar, of course, only some of the rules which people in fact observe, namely some of the rules of law (but never all, even of these) will be the product of deliberate design, while most of the rules of morals and custom will be spontaneous growths.

That even an order which rests on made rules may be spontaneous in character is shown by the fact that its particular manifestation will always depend on many circumstances which the designer of these rules did not and could not know. The particular content of the order will depend on the concrete circumstances known only to the individuals who obey the rules and apply them to facts known only to them. It will be through the knowledge of these individuals both of the rules and of the particular facts that both will determine the resulting order.

The spontaneous order of society is made up of individuals and organizations

In any group of men of more than the smallest size, collaboration will always rest both on spontaneous order as well as on deliberate organization. There is no doubt that for many limited tasks organization is the most powerful method of effective co-ordination because it enables us to adapt the resulting order much more fully to our wishes, while where, because of the complexity of the circumstances to be taken into account, we must rely on the forces making for a spontaneous order, our power over the particular contents of this order is necessarily restricted.

That the two kinds of order will regularly coexist in every society of any degree of complexity does not mean, however, that we can combine them in any manner we like. What in fact we find in all free societies is that, although groups of men will join in organizations for the achievement of some particular ends, the co-ordination of the activities of all these separate organizations, as well as of the separate individuals, is brought about by the forces making for a spontaneous order. The family, the farm, the plant, the firm, the corporation and the various associations, and all the public institutions including government, are organizations which in turn are integrated into a more comprehensive spontaneous order. It is advisable to reserve the term 'society' for this spontaneous overall order so that we may distinguish it from all the organized smaller groups which will exist within it, as well as from such smaller and more or less isolated groups as the horde, the tribe, or the clan, whose members will at least in some respects act under a central direction for common purposes. In some instances it will be the same group which at times, as when engaged in most of its daily routine, will operate as a spontaneous order maintained by the observation of conventional rules without the necessity of commands, while at other times, as when hunting, migrating, or fighting, it will be acting as an organization under the directing will of a chief.

The spontaneous order which we call a society also need not have such sharp boundaries as an organization will usually possess. There will often be a nucleus, or several nuclei, of more closely related individuals occupying a central position in a more loosely connected but more extensive order. Such particular societies within the Great Society may arise as the result of spatial proximity, or of some other special circumstances which produce closer relations among their members. And different partial societies of this sort will often overlap and every individual may, in addition to being a member of the Great Society, be a member of numerous other spontaneous sub-orders or partial societies of this sort as well as of various organizations existing within the comprehensive Great Society.

Of the organizations existing within the Great Society one which regularly occupies a very special position will be that which we call government. Although it is conceivable that the spontaneous order which we call society may exist without government, if the minimum of rules required for the formation of such an order is observed without an organized apparatus for their enforcement, in most circumstances the organization which we call government becomes indispensable in order to assure that those rules are obeyed.

This particular function of government is somewhat like that of a maintenance squad of a factory, its object being not to produce any particular services or products to be consumed by the citizens, but rather to see that the mechanism which regulates the production of those goods and services is kept in working order. The purposes for which this machinery is currently being used will be determined by those who operate its parts and in the last resort by those who buy its products.

The same organization that is charged with keeping in order an operating structure which the individuals will use for their own purposes, will, however, in addition to the task of enforcing the rules on which that order rests, usually be expected also to render other services which the spontaneous order cannot produce adequately. These two distinct functions of government are usually not clearly separated; yet, as we shall see, the distinction between the coercive functions in which government enforces rules of conduct, and its service functions in which it need merely administer resources placed at its disposal, is of fundamental importance. In the second it is one organization among many and like the others part of a spontaneous overall order, while in the first it provides an essential condition for the preservation of that overall order.

In English it is possible, and has long been usual, to discuss these two types of order in terms of the distinction between 'society' and 'government'. There is no need in the discussion of these problems, so long as only one country is concerned, to bring in the metaphysically charged term 'state'. It is largely under the influence of continental and particularly Hegelian thought that in the course of the last hundred years the practice of speaking of the 'state' (preferably with a capital 'S'), where 'government' is more appropriate and precise, has come to be widely adopted. That which acts, or pursues a policy, is however always the organization of government; and it does not make for clarity to drag in the term 'state' where 'government' is quite sufficient. It becomes particularly misleading when 'the state' rather than 'government' is contrasted with 'society' to indicate that the first is an organization and the second a spontaneous order.

The rules of spontaneous orders and the rules of organization

One of our chief contentions will be that, though spontaneous order and organization will always coexist, it is still not possible to mix these two principles of order in any manner we like. If this is not more generally understood it is due to the fact that for the determination of both kinds of order we have to rely on rules, and that the important differences between the kinds of rules which the two different kinds of order require are generally not recognized.

To some extent every organization must rely also on rules and not only on specific commands. The reason here is the same as that which makes it necessary for a spontaneous order to rely solely on rules: namely that by guiding the actions of individuals by rules rather than specific commands it is possible to make use of knowledge which nobody possesses as a whole. Every organization in which the members are not mere tools of the organizer will determine by commands only the function to be performed by each member, the purposes to be achieved, and certain general aspects of the methods to be employed, and will leave the detail to be decided by the individuals on the basis of their respective knowledge and skills.

Organization encounters here the problem which any attempt to bring order into complex human activities meets: the organizer must wish the individuals who are to co-operate to make use of knowledge that he himself does not possess. In none but the most simple kind of organization is it conceivable that all the details of all activities are governed by a single mind. Certainly nobody has yet succeeded in deliberately arranging all the activities that go on in a complex society. If anyone did ever succeed in fully organizing such a society, it would no longer make use of many minds but would be altogether dependent on one mind; it would certainly not be very complex but extremely primitive—and so would soon be the mind whose knowledge and will determined everything. The facts which could enter into the design of such an order could be only those which were known and digested by this mind; and as only he could decide on action and thus gain experience, there would be none of that interplay of many minds in which alone mind can grow.

What distinguishes the rules which will govern action within an organization is that they must be rules for the performance of assigned tasks. They presuppose that the place of each individual in a fixed structure is determined by command and that the rules each individual must obey depend on the place which he has been assigned and on the particular ends which have been indicated for him by the commanding authority. The rules will thus regulate merely the detail of the action of appointed functionaries or agencies of government.

Rules of organization are thus necessarily subsidiary to commands, filling in the gaps left by the commands. Such rules will be different for the different members of the organization according to the different roles which have been assigned to them, and they will have to be interpreted in the light of the purposes determined by the commands. Without the assignment of a function and the determination of the ends to be pursued by particular commands, the bare abstract rule would not be sufficient to tell each individual what he must do.

By contrast, the rules governing a spontaneous order must be independent of purpose and be the same, if not necessarily for all members, at least for whole classes of members not individually designated by name. They must, as we shall see, be rules applicable to an unknown and indeterminable number of persons and instances. They will have to be applied by the individuals in the light of their respective knowledge and purposes; and their application will be independent of any common purpose, which the individual need not even know.

In the terms we have adopted this means that the general rules of law that a spontaneous order rests on aim at an abstract order, the particular or concrete content of which is not known or foreseen by anyone; while the commands as well as the rules which govern an organization serve particular results aimed at by those who are in command of the organization. The more complex the order aimed at, the greater will be that part of the separate actions which will have to be determined by circumstances not known to those who direct the whole, and the more dependent control will be on rules rather than on specific commands. In the most complex types of organizations, indeed, little more than the assignment of particular functions and the general aim will be determined by command of the supreme authority, while the performance of these functions will be regulated only by rules—yet by rules which at least to some degree are specific to the functions assigned to particular persons. Only when we pass from the biggest kind of organization, government, which as organization must still be dedicated to a circumscribed and determined set of specific purposes, to the overall order of the whole of society, do we find an order which relies solely on rules and is entirely spontaneous in character.

It is because it was not dependent on organization but grew up as a spontaneous order that the structure of modern society has attained that degree of complexity which it possesses and which far exceeds any that could have been achieved by deliberate organization. In fact, of course, the rules which made the growth of this complex order possible were initially not designed in expectation of that result; but those people who happened to adopt suitable rules developed a complex civilization which then often spread to others. To maintain that we must deliberately plan modern society because it has become so complex is therefore paradoxical, and the result of a complete misunderstanding of these circumstances. The fact is, rather, that we can preserve an order of such complexity not by the method of directing the members, but only indirectly by enforcing and improving the rules conducive to the formation of a spontaneous order.

We shall see that it is impossible, not only to replace the spontaneous order by organization and at the same time to utilize as much of the dispersed knowledge of all its members as possible, but also to improve or correct this order by interfering in it by direct commands. Such a combination of spontaneous order and organization it can never be rational to adopt. While it is sensible to supplement the commands determining an organization by subsidiary rules, and to use organizations as elements of a spontaneous order, it can never be advantageous to supplement the rules governing a spontaneous order by isolated and subsidiary commands concerning those activities where the actions are guided by the general rules of conduct. This is the gist of the argument against 'interference' or 'intervention' in the market order. The reason why such isolated commands requiring specific actions by members of the spontaneous order can never improve but must disrupt that order is that they will refer to a part of a system of interdependent actions determined by information and guided by purposes known only to the several acting persons but not to the directing authority. The spontaneous order arises from each element balancing all the various factors operating on it and by adjusting all its various actions to each other, a balance which will be destroyed if some of the actions are determined by another agency on the basis of different knowledge and in the service of different ends.

What the general argument against 'interference' thus amounts to is that, although we can endeavour to improve a spontaneous order by revising the general rules on which it rests, and can supplement its results by the efforts of various organizations, we cannot improve the results by specific commands that deprive its members of the possibility of using their knowledge for their purposes.

We will have to consider throughout this book how these two kinds of rules have provided the model for two altogether different conceptions of law and how this has brought it about that authors using the same word 'law' have in fact been speaking about different things. This comes out most clearly in the contrast we find throughout history between those to whom law and liberty were inseparable[11] and those to whom the two were irreconcilable. We find one great tradition extending from the ancient Greeks and Cicero[12] through the Middle Ages[13] to the classical liberals like John Locke, David Hume, Immanuel Kant[14] and the Scottish moral philosophers, down to various American statesmen[15] of the nineteenth and twentieth centuries, for whom law and liberty could not exist apart from each other; while to Thomas Hobbes, Jeremy Bentham[16] and many French thinkers[17] and the modern legal positivists law of necessity means an encroachment on freedom. This apparent conflict between long lines of great thinkers does not mean that they arrived at opposite conclusions, but merely that they were using the word 'law' in different senses.

The terms 'organism' and 'organization'

A few comments should be added on the terms in which the distinction examined in this chapter has most commonly been discussed in the past. Since the beginning of the nineteenth century the terms 'organism' and 'organization' have been frequently used to contrast the two types of order. As we have found it advisable to avoid the former term and to adopt the latter in a specific sense, some comments on their history may be appropriate.

It was natural that the organismal analogy should have been used since ancient times to describe the spontaneous order of society, since organisms were the only kinds of spontaneous order with which everybody was familiar. Organisms are indeed a kind of spontaneous order and as such show many of the characteristics of other spontaneous orders. It was therefore tempting to borrow such terms as 'growth', 'adaptation', and 'function' from them. They are, however, spontaneous orders of a very special kind, possessing also properties which by no means necessarily belong to all spontaneous orders; the analogy in consequence soon becomes more misleading than helpful.[18]

The chief peculiarity of organisms which distinguishes them from the spontaneous orders of society is that in an organism most of the individual elements occupy fixed places which, at least once the organism is mature, they retain once and for all. They also, as a rule, are more or less constant systems consisting of a fixed number of elements which, although some may be replaced by equivalent new ones, retain an order in space readily perceivable with the senses. They are, in consequence, in the terms we have used, orders of a more concrete kind than the spontaneous orders of society, which may be preserved although the total number of elements changes and the individual elements change their places. This relatively concrete character of the order of organisms shows itself in the fact that their existence as distinct wholes can be perceived intuitively by the senses, while the abstract spontaneous order of social structures usually can only be reconstructed by the mind.

The interpretation of society as an organism has almost invariably been used in support of hierarchic and authoritarian views to which the more general conception of the spontaneous order gives no support. Indeed, since Menenius Agrippa, on the occasion of the first secession of the Roman plebs, used the organismal metaphor to justify the privileges of a particular group, it must have been used innumerable times for similar purposes. The suggestion of fixed places assigned to particular elements according to their distinct 'functions', and the much more concrete determination of the biological structures as compared with the abstract character of the spontaneous structures of society, have indeed made the organismal conception of very questionable value for social theory. It has been abused even more than the term 'order' itself when interpreted as a made order or *taxis*, and has frequently been used to defend a hierarchical order, the necessity of 'degree', the relation of command and obedience, or the preservation of established positions of particular individuals, and for this reason has rightly become suspect.

The term 'organization', on the other hand, which in the nineteenth century was frequently used in contrast to 'organism' to express the distinction we have discussed, [19] and which we shall retain to describe a made order or *taxis*, is of comparatively recent origin. It seems to have come into general use at the time of the French Revolution, with reference to which Kant once observed that 'in a recently undertaken reconstruction of a great people into a great state the word *organization* has been frequently and appropriately used for the institution of the magistracies and even the whole state.' [20] The word became characteristic of the spirit of the Napoleonic period [21] and became the central conception in the plans for the 'reconstruction of society' of the chief founders of modern socialism, the Saint Simonians, and of Auguste Comte. [22] Until the term 'socialism' came into general, use 'the organization of society as a whole' was in fact the accepted way of referring to what we now describe as socialism.[23] Its central role, particularly for French thinking during the early part of the nineteenth century, was clearly seen by the young Ernest Renan, who in 1849 could speak of the ideal of a 'scientific organization of mankind as the last word of modern science and its daring but legitimate ambition'.[24]

In English, the word appears to have come into general use around 1790 as a technical term for a 'systematic arrangement for a definite purpose'.[25] But it was the Germans who adopted it with particular enthusiasm and to whom it soon appeared to express a peculiar capacity in which they believed themselves to excel other people. This even led to a curious rivalry between French and German scholars, who during the First World War conducted a slightly comic literary dispute across the fighting lines as to which of the two nations had the stronger claim to possessing the secret of organization.[26]

In confining the term here to a made order or *taxis* we follow what seems to have become the general use in sociology and especially in what is known as 'organization theory'.[27] The idea of organization in this sense is a natural consequence of the discovery of the powers of the human intellect and especially of the general attitude of constructivist rationalism. It appeared for a long time as the only procedure by which an order serviceable to human purposes could be deliberately achieved, and it is indeed the intelligent and powerful method of achieving certain known and forseeable results. But as its development is one of the great achievements of constructivism, so is the disregard of its limits one of its most serious defects. What it overlooks is that the growth of that mind which can direct an organization, and of the more comprehensive order within which organizations function, rests on adaptations to the unforeseeable, and that the only possibility of transcending the capacity of individual minds is to rely on those super-personal 'self-organizing' forces which create spontaneous orders.

THREE

PRINCIPLES AND EXPEDIENCY

The frequent recurrence to fundamental principles is
absolutely necessary to preserve the blessings of liberty.
Constitution of North Carolina*

Individual aims and collective benefits

The thesis of this book is that a condition of liberty in which all
are allowed to use their knowledge for their purposes, restrained
only by rules of just conduct of universal application, is likely to
produce for them the best conditions for achieving their aims; and
that such a system is likely to be achieved and maintained only if
all authority, including that of the majority of the people, is limited
in the exercise of coercive power by general principles to which the
community has committed itself. Individual freedom, wherever
it has existed, has been largely the product of a prevailing respect
for such principles which, however, have never been fully articulated in constitutional documents. Freedom has been preserved for
prolonged periods because such principles, vaguely and dimly perceived, have governed public opinion. The institutions by which the
countries of the Western world have attempted to protect individual
freedom against progressive encroachment by government have
always proved inadequate when transferred to countries where such
traditions did not prevail. And they have not provided sufficient
protection against the effects of new desires which even among the
peoples of the West now often loom larger than the older conceptions—conceptions that made possible the periods of freedom when
these peoples gained their present position.

I will not undertake here a fuller definition of the term 'freedom' or enlarge upon why we regard individual freedom as so important. That I have attempted in another book.[1] But a few words
should be said about why I prefer the short formula by which I
have repeatedly described the condition of freedom, namely a state

in which each can use his knowledge for his purposes, to the classic phrase of Adam Smith, 'every man, so long as he does not violate the laws of justice [being] left perfectly free to pursue his own interests in his own way.'[2] The reason for my preference is that the latter formula unnecessarily and unfortunately suggests, without intending to, a connection of the argument for individual freedom with egotism or selfishness. The freedom to pursue his own aims is, however, at least as important for the complete altruist as for the most selfish. Altruism, to be a virtue, certainly does not presuppose that one has to follow another person's will. But it is true that much pretended altruism manifests itself in a desire to make others serve the ends which the 'altruist' regards as important.

We need not return here to the undeniable fact that the beneficial effects on others of one's efforts will often become visible to one only if one acts as part of a concerted effort of many in accordance with a coherent plan, and that it may often be difficult for the isolated individual to do much about the evils that deeply concern him. But it is, of course, part of his freedom that for such purposes he can join (or create) organizations which will enable him to take part in concerted action. And though some of the ends of the altruist will be achievable only by collective action, purely selfish ends too will as often be achieved through it. There is no necessary connection between altruism and collective action, or between egotism and individual action.

Freedom can be preserved only by following principles and is destroyed by following expediency

From the insight that the benefits of civilization rest on the use of more knowledge than can be used in any deliberately concerted effort, it follows that it is not in our power to build a desirable society by simply putting together the particular elements that by themselves appear desirable. Although probably all beneficial improvement must be piecemeal, if the separate steps are not guided by a body of coherent principles, the outcome is likely to be a suppression of individual freedom.

The reason for this is very simple, although not generally understood. Since the value of freedom rests on the opportunities it provides for unforeseen and unpredictable actions, we will rarely know what we lose through a particular restriction of freedom. Any such restriction, any coercion other than the enforcement of general rules, will aim at the achievement of some foreseeable particular result, but what is prevented by it will usually not be known. The direct effects of any interference with the market order will be near and clearly visible in most cases, while the more indirect and remote effects will mostly be unknown and will therefore be disregarded. [3] We shall never be aware of all the costs of achieving particular results by such interference.

And so, when we decide each issue solely on what appear to be its individual merits, we always over-estimate the advantages of central direction. Our choice will regularly appear to be one between a certain known and tangible gain and the mere probability of the prevention of some unknown beneficial action by unknown persons. If the choice between freedom and coercion is thus treated as a matter of expediency, [4] freedom is bound to be sacrificed in almost every instance. As in the particular instance we shall hardly ever know what would be the consequence of allowing people to make their own choice, to make the decision in each instance depend only on the foreseeable particular results must lead to the progressive destruction of freedom. There are probably few restrictions on freedom which could not be justified on the grounds that we do not know the particular loss they will cause.

That freedom can be preserved only if it is treated as a supreme principle which must not be sacrificed for particular advantages was fully understood by the leading liberal thinkers of the nineteenth century, one of whom even described liberalism as 'the system of principles'. [5] Such is the chief burden of their warnings concerning 'What is seen and what is not seen in political economy' [6] and about the 'pragmatism that contrary to the intentions of its representatives inexorably leads to socialism'. [7]

All these warnings were, however, thrown to the wind, and the progressive discarding of principles and the increasing determination during the last hundred years to proceed pragmatically [8] is one of the most important innovations in social and economic policy. That we should foreswear all principles or 'isms' in order to achieve greater mastery over our fate is even now proclaimed as the new wisdom of our age. Applying to each task the 'social techniques' most appropriate to its solution, unfettered by any dogmatic belief, seems to some the only manner of proceeding worthy of a rational and scientific age. [9] 'Ideologies', that is sets of principles, have become generally as unpopular as they have always been with aspiring dictators such as Napoleon I or Karl Marx, the two men who gave the word its modern derogatory meaning.

If I am not mistaken, this fashionable contempt for 'ideology', or for all general principles or 'isms', is a characteristic attitude of disillusioned socialists who, because they have been forced by the inherent contradictions of their own ideology to discard it, have concluded that all ideologies must be erroneous and that in order to be rational one must do without one. But to be guided only, as they imagine it to be possible, by explicit particular purposes which one consciously accepts, and to reject all general values whose conduciveness to particular desirable results cannot be demonstrated (or to be guided only by what Max Weber calls 'purposive rationality') is an impossibility. Although, admittedly, an ideology is something which cannot be 'proved' (or demonstrated to be true), it may well be something whose widespread acceptance is the indispensable condition for most of the particular things we strive for.

Those self-styled modern 'realists' have only contempt for the old-fashioned reminder that if one starts unsystematically to interfere with the spontaneous order there is no practicable halting point and that it is therefore necessary to choose between alternative systems. They are pleased to think that by proceeding experimentally and therefore 'scientifically' they will succeed in fitting together in piecemeal fashion a desirable order by choosing for each particular desired result what science shows them to be the most appropriate means of achieving it.

Since warnings against this sort of procedure have often been misunderstood, as one of my earlier books has, a few more words about their intentions may be appropriate. What I meant to argue in *The Road to Serfdom*[10] was certainly not that whenever we depart, however slightly, from what I regard as the principles of a free society, we shall ineluctably be driven to go the whole way to a totalitarian system. It was rather what in more homely language is expressed when we say: 'If you do not mend your principles you will go to the devil.' That this has often been understood to describe a necessary process over which we have no power once we have embarked on it, is merely an indication of how little the importance of principles for the determination of policy is understood, and particularly how completely overlooked is the fundamental fact that by our political actions we unintentionally produce the acceptance of principles which will make further action necessary.

What is overlooked by those unrealistic modern 'realists' who pride themselves on the modernity of their view is that they are advocating something which most of the Western world has indeed been doing for the past two or three generations, and which is responsible for the conditions of present politics. The end of the liberal era of principles might well be dated at the time when, more than eighty years ago, W. S. Jevons pronounced that in economic and social policy 'we can lay down no hard and fast rules, but must treat every case in detail upon its merits.'[11] Ten years later Herbert Spencer could already speak of 'the reigning school of politics' by whom 'nothing less than scorn is shown for every doctrine which implies restraints on the doings of immediate expediency' or which relies on 'abstract principles'.[12]

This 'realistic' view which has now dominated politics for so long has hardly produced the results which its advocates desired. Instead of having achieved greater mastery over our fate we find ourselves in fact more frequently committed to a path which we have not deliberately chosen, and faced with 'inevitable necessities' of further action which, though never intended, are the result of what we have done.

The 'necessities' of policy are generally the consequences of earlier measures

The contention often advanced that certain political measures were inevitable has a curious double aspect. With regard to developments that are approved by those who employ this argument, it is readily accepted and used in justification of the actions. But when developments take an undesirable turn, the suggestion that this is not the effect of circumstances beyond our control, but the necessary consequence of our earlier decisions, is rejected with scorn. The idea that we are not fully free to pick and choose whatever combination of features we wish our society to possess, or to fit them together into a viable whole, that is, that we cannot build a desirable social order like a mosaic by selecting whatever particular parts we like best, and that many well-intentioned measures may have a long train of unforeseeable and undesirable consequences, seems to be intolerable to modern man. He has been taught that what he has made he can also alter at will to suit his wishes, and conversely, that what he can alter he must also have made in the first instance. He has not yet learnt that this naïve belief derives from that ambiguity of the word 'made' which we discussed earlier.

In fact, of course, the chief circumstance which will make

certain measures seem unavoidable is usually the result of our past actions and of the opinions which are now held. Most of the 'necessities' of policy are of our own creation. I am myself now old enough to have been told more than once by my elders that certain consequences of their policy which I foresaw would never occur, and later, when they did appear, to have been told by younger men that these had been inevitable and quite independent of what in fact was done.

The reason why we cannot achieve a coherent whole by just fitting together any elements we like is that the appropriateness of any particular arrangement within a spontaneous order will depend on all the rest of it, and that any particular change we make in it will tell us little about how it would operate in a different setting. An experiment can tell us only whether any innovation does or does not fit into a given framework. But to hope that we can build a coherent order by random experimentation with particular solutions of individual problems and without following guiding principles is an illusion. Experience tells us much about the effectiveness of different social and economic systems as a whole. But an order of the complexity of modern society can be designed neither as a whole, nor by shaping each part separately without regard to the rest, but only by consistently adhering to certain principles throughout a process of evolution.

This is not to say that these 'principles' must necessarily take the form of articulated rules. Principles are often more effective guides for action when they appear as no more than an unreasoned prejudice, a general feeling that certain things simply 'are not done'; while as soon as they are explicity stated speculation begins about their correctness and their validity. It is probably true that in the eighteenth century the English, little given to speculation about general principles, were for this reason much more firmly guided by strong opinions about what kinds of political actions were permissible, than the French who tried so hard to discover and adopt such principles. Once the instinctive certainty is lost, perhaps as a result of unsuccessful attempts to put into words principles that had been observed 'intuitively', there is no way of regaining such guidance other than to search for a correct statement of what before was known implicitly.

The impression that the English in the seventeen and eighteenth centuries, through their gift of 'muddling through' and their 'genius for compromise', succeeded in building up a viable system without talking much about principles, while the French, with all their concern about explicit assumptions and clear formulations, never did so, may thus be misleading. The truth seems to be that while they talked little about principles, the English were much more surely guided by principles, while in France the very speculation about basic principles prevented any one set of principles from taking a firm hold.

The danger of attaching greater importance to the predictable rather than to the merely possible consequences of our actions

The preservation of a free system is so difficult precisely because it requires a constant rejection of measures which appear to be required to secure particular results, on no stronger grounds than that they conflict with a general rule, and frequently without our knowing what will be the costs of not observing the rule in the particular instance. A successful defence of freedom must therefore be dogmatic and make no concessions to expediency, even where it is not possible to show that, besides the known beneficial effects, some particular harmful result would also follow from its infringement. Freedom will prevail only if it is accepted as a general principle whose application to particular instances requires no justification. It is thus a misunderstanding to blame classical liberalism for having been too doctrinaire. Its defect was not that it adhered too stubbornly to principles, but rather that it lacked principles sufficiently definite to provide clear guidance, and that it often appeared simply to accept the traditional functions of government and to oppose all new ones. Consistency is possible only if definite principles are accepted. But the concept of liberty with which the liberals of the nineteenth century operated was in many respects so vague that it did not provide clear guidance.

People will not refrain from those restrictions on individual liberty that appear to them the simplest and most direct remedy of a recognized evil, if there does not prevail a strong belief in definite principles. The loss of such belief and the preference for expediency is in part a result of the fact that we no longer have any principles which can be rationally defended. The rules of thumb which at one time were accepted were not adequate to decide what is and what is not permissible in a free system. We have no longer even a generally understood name for what the term 'free system' only vaguely describes. Certainly neither 'capitalism' nor *laissez-*

faire properly describe it; and both terms are understandably more popular with the enemies than with the defenders of a free system. 'Capitalism' is an appropriate name at most for the partial realization of such a system in a certain historical phase, but always misleading because it suggests a system which mainly benefits the capitalists, while in fact it is a system which imposes upon enterprise a discipline under which the managers chafe and which each endeavours to escape. *Laissez-faire* was never more than a rule of thumb. It indeed expressed protest against abuses of governmental power, but never provided a criterion by which one could decide what were the proper functions of government. Much the same applies to the terms 'free enterprise' or 'market economy' which, without a definition of the free sphere of the individual, say little. The expression 'liberty under the law', which at one time perhaps conveyed the essential point better than any other, has become almost meaningless because both 'liberty' and 'law' no longer have a clear meaning. And the only term that in the past was widely and correctly understood, namely 'liberalism', has 'as a supreme but unintended compliment been appropriated by the opponents of this ideal'.[13]

The lay reader may not be fully aware how much we have already moved away from the ideal expressed by those terms. While the lawyer or political scientist will at once see that what I shall be espousing is an ideal that has largely vanished and has never been fully realized, it is probably true that the majority of people believe that something like it still governs public affairs. It is because we have departed from the ideal so much further than most people realize, and because, unless this development is soon checked, it will by its own momentum transform society from a free into a totalitarian one, that we must reconsider the general principles guiding our political actions. We are still as free as we are because certain traditional but rapidly vanishing prejudices have impeded the process by which the inherent logic of the changes we have already made tends to assert itself in an ever widening field. In the present state of opinion the ultimate victory of totalitarianism would indeed be no more than the final victory of the ideas already dominant in the intellectual sphere over a merely traditionalist resistance.

Spurious realism and the required courage to consider utopia

With respect to policy, the methodological insight that in the case of complex spontaneous orders we will never be able to determine more than the general principles on which they operate or to predict the particular changes that any event in the environment will bring about, has far-reaching consequences. It means that where we rely on spontaneous ordering forces we shall often not be able to foresee the particular changes by which the necessary adaptation to altered external circumstances will be brought about, and sometimes perhaps not even be able to conceive in what manner the restoration of a disturbed 'equilibrium' or 'balance' can be accomplished. This ignorance of how the mechanism of the spontaneous order will solve such a 'problem' which we know must be solved somehow if the overall order is not to disintegrate, often produces a panic-like alarm and the demand for government action for the restoration of the disturbed balance.

Often it is even the acquisition of a partial insight into the character of the spontaneous overall order that becomes the cause of the demands for deliberate control. So long as the balance of trade, or the correspondence of supply and demand of any particular commodity, adjusted itself spontaneously after any disturbance, men rarely asked themselves how this happened. But, once they became aware of the necessity of such constant readjustments, they felt that somebody must be made responsible for deliberately bringing them about. The economist, from the very nature of his schematic picture of the spontaneous order, could counter such apprehension only by the confident assertion that the required new balance would establish itself somehow if we did not interfere with the spontaneous forces; but, as he is usually unable to predict precisely how this would happen, his assertions were not very convincing.

Yet when it is possible to foresee how the spontaneous forces are likely to restore the disturbed balance, the situation becomes even worse. The necessity of adaptation to unforeseen events will always mean that someone is going to be hurt, that someone's expectations will be disappointed or his efforts frustrated. This leads to the demand that the required adjustment be brought about by deliberate guidance, which in practice must mean that authority is to decide who is to be hurt. The effect of this is often that necessary adjustments will be prevented whenever they can be foreseen.

What helpful insight science can provide for the guidance of policy consists in an understanding of the general nature of the spontaneous order, and not in any knowledge of the particulars of a concrete situation, which it does not and cannot possess. The true appreciation of what science has to contribute to the solution of our political tasks, which in the nineteenth century was fairly general, has been obscured by the new tendency derived from a now fashionable misconception of the nature of scientific method: the belief that science consists of a collection of particular observed facts, which is erroneous so far as science in general is concerned, but doubly misleading where we have to deal with the parts of a complex spontaneous order. Since all the events in any part of such an order are interdependent, and an abstract order of this sort has no recurrent concrete parts which can be identified by individual attributes, it is necessarily vain to try to discover by observation regularities in any of its parts. The only theory which in this field can lay claim to scientific status is the theory of the order as a whole; and such a theory (although it has, of course, to be tested on the facts) can never be achieved inductively by observation but only through constructing mental models made up from the observable elements.

The myopic view of science that concentrates on the study of particular facts because they alone are empirically observable, and whose advocates even pride themselves on not being guided by such a conception of the overall order as can be obtained only by what they call 'abstract speculation', by no means increases our power of shaping a desirable order, but in fact deprives us of all effective guidance for successful action. The spurious 'realism' which deceives itself in believing that it can dispense with any guiding conception of the nature of the overall order, and confines itself to an examination of particular 'techniques' for achieving particular results, is in reality highly unrealistic. Especially when this attitude leads, as it frequently does, to a judgment of the advisability of particular measures by consideration of the 'practicability' in the given political climate of opinion, it often tends merely to drive us further into an impasse. Such must be the ultimate results of successive measures which all tend to destroy the overall order that their advocates at the same time tacitly assume to exist.

It is not to be denied that to some extent the guiding model of the overall order will always be an utopia, something to which the existing situation will be only a distant approximation and which many people will regard as wholly impractical. Yet it is only by constantly holding up the guiding conception of an internally consistent model which could be realized by the consistent application of the same principles, that anything like an effective framework for a functioning spontaneous order will be achieved. Adam Smith thought that 'to expect, indeed, that freedom of trade should ever be entirely restored in Great Britain is as absurd as to expect an Oceana or Utopia should ever be established in it.'[14] Yet seventy year later, largely as a result of his work, it was achieved.

Utopia, like ideology, is a bad word today; and it is true that most utopias aim at radically redesigning society and suffer from internal contradictions which make their realization impossible. But an ideal picture of a society which may not be wholly achievable, or a guiding conception of the overall order to be aimed at, is nevertheless not only the indispensable precondition of any rational policy, but also the chief contribution that science can make to the solution of the problems of practical policy.

The role of the lawyer in political evolution

The chief instrument of deliberate change in modern society is legislation. But however carefully we may think out beforehand every single act of law-making, we are never free to redesign completely the legal system as a whole, or to remake it out of the whole cloth according to a coherent design. Law-making is necessarily a continuous process in which every step produces hitherto unforeseen consequences for what we can or must do next. The parts of a legal system are not so much adjusted to each other according to a comprehensive overall view, as gradually adapted to each other by the successive application of general principles to particular problems—principles, that is, which are often not even explicitly known but merely implicit in the particular measures that are taken. For those who imagine it possible to arrange deliberately all the particular activities of a Great Society according to a coherent plan, it should indeed be a sobering reflection that this has not proved possible even for such a part of the whole as the system of law. Few facts show more clearly how prevailing conceptions will bring about a continuous change, producing measures that in the beginning nobody had desired or foreseen but which appear inevitable in due course, than the process of the change of law. Every single step in this process is determined by problems that arise when the principles laid down by (or implicit in) earlier decisions are applied to circumstances which were then not foreseen. There is nothing specially mysterious about these 'inner dynamics of the law' which produce change not willed as a whole by anybody.

In this process the individual lawyer is necessarily more an unwitting tool, a link in a chain of events that he does not see as a whole, than a conscious initiator. Whether he acts as a judge or as the drafter of a statute, the framework of general conceptions into which we must fit his decision is given to him, and his task is to apply these general principles of the law, not to question them. However much he may be concerned about the future implications of his decisions, he can judge them only in the context of all the other recognized principles of the law that are given to him. This is, of course, as it ought to be; it is of the essence of legal thinking and of just decisions that the lawyer strives to make the whole system consistent.

It is often said that the professional bias of the lawyer is conservative. [15] In certain conditions, namely when some basic principles of the law have been accepted for a long time, they will indeed govern the whole system of law, its general spirit as well as every single rule and application within it. At such times it will possess great inherent stability. Every lawyer will, when he has to interpret or apply a rule which is not in accord with the rest of the system, endeavour so to bend it as to make it conform with the others. The legal profession as a whole may thus occasionally in effect even nullify the intention of the legislator, not out of disrespect for the law, but, on the contrary, because their technique leads them to give preference to what is still the predominant part of the law and to fit an alien element into it by so transforming it as to make it harmonize with the whole.

The situation is entirely different, however, when a general philosophy of the law which is not in accord with the greater part of the existing law has recently gained ascendancy. The same lawyers will, through the same habits and techniques, and generally as unwittingly, become a revolutionary force, as effective in transforming the law down to every detail as they were before in preserving it. The same forces which in the first condition make for lack of movement, will in the second tend to accelerate change until it has transformed the whole body of law much beyond the point that anyone foresaw or desired. Whether this process will lead to a new equilibrium or to a disintegration of the whole body of law in the sense in which we still chiefly understand the word, will depend on the character of the new philosophy.

We live in such a period of transformation of the law by inner forces and it is submitted that, if the principles which at present guide that process are allowed to work themselves out to their logical consequences, law as we know it as the chief protection of the freedom of the individual is bound to disappear. Already the lawyers in many fields have, as the instrument of a general conception which they have not made, become the tools, not of principles of justice, but of an apparatus in which the individual is made to serve the ends of his rulers. Legal thinking appears already to be governed to such an extent by new conceptions of the functions of law that, if these conceptions were consistently applied, the whole system of rules of individual conduct would be transformed into a system of rules of organization.

These developments have indeed been noticed with apprehension by many professional lawyers whose chief concern is still with what is sometimes described as 'lawyer's law', that is, those rules of just conduct which at one time were regarded as *the* law. But the leadership in jurisprudence, in the course of the process we have described, has shifted from the practitioners of private law to the public lawyer, with the result that today the philosophical preconceptions which govern the development of all law, including the private law, are almost entirely fashioned by men whose main concern is the public law or the rules of organization of government.

The modern development of law has been guided largely by false economics

It would, however, be unjust to blame the lawyers for this state of affairs more than the economists. The practising lawyer will indeed in general best perform his task if he just applies the general principles of the law which he has learned and which it is his duty consistently to apply. It is only in the theory of law, in the formulation and elaboration of those general principles, that the basic problem of their relation to a viable order of actions arises. For such a formulation and elaboration, an understanding of this order is absolutely essential if any intelligent choice between alternative principles is to be made. During the last two or three generations, however, a misunderstanding rather than an understanding of the character of this order has guided legal philosophy.

The economists in their turn, at least after the time of David Hume and Adam Smith, who were also philosophers of law, certainly showed no more appreciation of the significance of the system of legal rules, the existence of which was tacitly presupposed by their argument. They rarely put their account of the determination of a spontaneous order in a form which could be of much use to the legal theorist. But they have probably contributed unknowingly as much to the transformation of the whole social order as the lawyers have done.

This becomes evident when we examine the reason regularly given by the lawyers for the great changes that the character of law has undergone during the last hundred years. Everywhere, whether it be in English or American, French or German legal literature, we find alleged economic necessities given as the reasons for these changes. To the economist, reading the account by which the lawyers explain that transformation of the law, is a somewhat melancholy experience: he finds all the sins of his predecessors visited upon him. Accounts of the modern development of law are full of references to 'irreversible compelling forces' and 'inevitable tendencies' which are alleged to have imperatively called for the particular changes. The fact that 'all modern democracies' did this or that is adduced as proof of the wisdom or necessity of such changes.

These accounts invariably speak of a past *laissez-faire* period, as if there had been a time when no efforts were made to improve the legal framework so as to make the market operate more beneficially or to supplement its results. Almost without exception they base their argument on the *fable convenue* that free enterprise has operated to the disadvantage of the manual workers, and allege that 'early capitalism' or 'liberalism' had brought about a decline in the material standard of the working class. The legend, although wholly untrue, [16] has become part of the folklore of our time. The fact is, of course, that as the result of the growth of free markets, the reward of manual labour has during the past hundred and fifty years experienced an increase unknown in any earlier period of history. Most contemporary works on legal philosophy are full also of outdated clichés about the alleged self-destructive tendency of competition, or the need for 'planning' created by the increased complexity of the modern world, clichés deriving from the high tide of enthusiasm for 'planning' of thirty or forty years ago, when it was widely accepted and its totalitarian implications not yet clearly understood.

It is indeed doubtful whether as much false economics has been spread during the last hundred years by any other means as by the teaching of the young lawyers by their elders that 'it was necessary' this or that should have been done, or that such and such circumstances 'made it inevitable' that certain measures should be taken. It seems almost to be a habit of thought of the lawyer to regard the fact that the legislature has decided on something as evidence of the wisdom of that decision. This means, however, that his efforts will be beneficial or pernicious according to the wisdom or foolishness of the precedents by which he is guided, and that he is as likely to become the perpetuator of the errors as of the wisdom of the past. If he accepts as mandatory for him the observable trend of development, he is as likely to become simply the instrument through which changes he does not understand work themselves out as the conscious creator of a new order. In such a condition it will be necessary to seek for criteria of the desirability of developments elsewhere than within the science of law.

This is not to say that economics alone provides the principles that ought to guide legislation—although considering the influence that economic conceptions inevitably exercise, one must wish that such influence would come from good economics and not from that collection of myths and fables about economic development which seem today to govern legal thinking. Our contention is rather that the principles and preconceptions which guide the development of law inevitably come in part from outside the law and can be beneficial only if they are based on a true conception about how the activities in a Great Society can be effectively ordered.

The role of the lawyer in social evolution and the manner in which his actions are determined are indeed the best illustration of a truth of fundamental importance: namely that, whether we want it or not, the decisive factors which will determine that evolution will always be highly abstract and often unconsciously held ideas about what is right and proper, and not particular purposes or concrete desires. It is not so much what men consciously aim at, as their opinions about permissible methods, which determine not only what will be done but also whether anyone will have the power of doing it. This is the message reiterated by the greatest students of social affairs and always disregarded, namely that 'though men be much more governed by interest yet even interest itself, and all human affairs, are entirely governed by *opinion*.'[17]

Few contentions meet with such disbelief from most practical men, and are so much disregarded by the dominant school of political thought, as that, what is contemptuously dubbed as an ideology, has dominant power over those who believe themselves to be free from it even more than over those who consciously embrace it. Yet there are few things which must impress themselves more strongly on the student of the evolution of social institutions than the fact that what decisively determines them are not good or bad intentions concerning their immediate consequences, but the general preconceptions in terms of which particular issues are decided.

The power of abstract ideas rests largely on the very fact that they are not consciously held as theories but are treated by most people as self-evident truths which act as tacit presuppositions. That this dominant power of ideas is so rarely admitted is largely due to the oversimplified manner in which it is often asserted, suggesting that some great mind had the power of impressing on succeeding generations their particular conceptions. But which ideas will dominate, mostly without people ever being aware of them, is, of course, determined by a slow and immensely intricate process which we can rarely reconstruct in outline even in retrospect. It is certainly humbling to have to admit that our present decisions are determined by what happened long ago in a remote specialty without the general public ever knowing about it, and without those who first formulated the new conception being aware of what would be its consequences, particularly when it was not a discovery of new facts but a general philosophical conception which later affected particular decisions. These opinions not only the 'men in the street', but also the experts in the particular fields, accept unreflectingly and in general simply because they happen to be 'modern'.

It is necessary to realize that the sources of many of the most harmful agents in this world are often not evil men but highminded idealists, and that in particular the foundations of totalitarian barbarism have been laid by honourable and well-meaning scholars who never recognized the offspring they produced.[18] The fact is that, especially in the legal field, certain guiding philosophical preconceptions have brought about a situation where well-meaning theorists, highly admired to the present day even in free countries, have already worked out all the basic conceptions of a totalitarian order. Indeed, the communists, no less than the fascists or national socialists, had merely to use conceptions provided by generations of legal theorists in order to arrive at their doctrines.

What concerns us here is, however, not so much the past as the present. In spite of the collapse of the totalitarian regimes in the western world, their basic ideas have in the theoretical sphere continued to gain ground, so much so that to transform completely the legal system into a totalitarian one all that is needed now is to allow the ideas already reigning in the abstract sphere to be translated into practice.

Nowhere can this situation be more clearly seen than in Germany, which not only has largely provided the rest of the world with the philosophical conceptions that have produced the totalitarian regimes, but which also has been one of the first to succumb to this product of conceptions nurtured in the abstract sphere. Although the average German has by his experience probably been thoroughly purged of any conscious leaning towards the recognizable manifestations of totalitarianism, the basic philosophical conceptions have merely retreated into the abstract sphere, and now lurk in the hearts of grave and highly respected scholars, ready, unless discredited in time, again to take control of developments.

There is indeed no better illustration or more explicit statement of the manner in which philosophical conceptions about the nature of the social order affect the development of law than the theories of Carl Schmitt who, long before Hitler came to power, directed all his formidable intellectual energies to a fight against liberalism in all its forms;[19] who then became one of Hitler's chief legal apologists and still enjoys great influence among German legal philosophers and public lawyers; and whose characteristic terminology is as readily employed by German socialists as by conservative philosophers. His central belief, as he finally formulated it, is that from the 'normative' thinking of the liberal tradition law has gradually advanced through a 'decisionist' phase in which the will of the legislative authorities decided on particular matters, to the conception of a 'concrete order formation', a development which involves 'a re-interpretation of the ideal of the *nomos* as a total conception of law importing a concrete order and community'.[20] In other words, law is not to consist of abstract rules which make possible the formation of a spontaneous order by the free action of individuals through limiting the range of their actions, but is to be the instrument of arrangement or organization by which the individual is made to serve concrete purposes. This is the inevitable outcome of an intellectual development in which the self-ordering forces of society and the role of law in an ordering mechanism are no longer understood.

FOUR

THE CHANGING CONCEPT OF LAW

Non ex regula ius sumatur, sed ex iure quod est regula fiat.

Julius Paulus*

Law is older than legislation

Legislation, the deliberate making of law, has justly been described as among all inventions of man the one fraught with the gravest consequences, more far-reaching in its effects even than fire and gun-powder. [1] Unlike law itself, which has never been 'invented' in the same sense, the invention of legislation came relatively late in the history of mankind. It gave into the hands of men an instrument of great power which they needed to achieve some good, but which they have not yet learned so to control that it may not produce great evil. It opened to man wholly new possibilities and gave him a new sense of power over his fate. The discussion about who should possess this power has, however, unduly overshadowed the much more fundamental question of how far this power should extend. It will certainly remain an exceedingly dangerous power so long as we believe that it will do harm only if wielded by bad men. [2]

Law in the sense of enforced rules of conduct is undoubtedly coeval with society; only the observance of common rules makes the peaceful existence of individuals in society possible. [3] Long before man had developed language to the point where it enabled him to issue general commands, an individual would be accepted as a member of a group only so long as he conformed to its rules. Such rules might in a sense not be known and still have to be discovered, because from 'knowing how' to act, [4] or from being able to recognize that the acts of another did or did not conform to accepted practices, it is still a long way to being able to state such rules in words. But while it might be generally recognized that the discovery and statement of what the accepted rules were (or the articulation of rules that would be approved when acted upon) was a task requiring special wisdom, nobody yet conceived of law as something which men could make at will.

It is no accident that we still use the same word 'law' for the invariable rules which govern nature and for the rules which govern men's conduct. They were both conceived at first as something existing independently of human will. Though the anthropomorphic tendencies of all primitive thinking made men often ascribe both kinds of law to the creation of some supernatural being, they were regarded as eternal truths that man could try to discover but which he could not alter.

To modern man, on the other hand, the belief that all law governing human action is the product of legislation appears so obvious that the contention that law is older than law-making has almost the character of a paradox. Yet there can be no doubt that law existed for ages before it occurred to man that he could make or alter it. The belief that he could do so appeared hardly earlier than in classical Greece and even then only to be submerged again and to reappear and gradually gain wider acceptance in the later Middle Ages. [5] In the form in which it is now widely held, however, namely that all law is, can be, and ought to be, the product of the free invention of a legislator, it is factually false, an erroneous product of that constructivist rationalism which we described earlier.

We shall later see that the whole conception of legal positivism which derives all law from the will of a legislator is a product of the intentionalist fallacy characteristic of constructivism, a relapse into those design theories of human institutions which stand in irreconcilable conflict with all we know about the evolution of law and most other human institutions.

What we know about pre-human and primitive human societies suggests a different origin and determination of law from that assumed by the theories which trace it to the will of a legislator. And although the positivist doctrine stands also in flagrant conflict with what we know about the history of our law, legal history proper begins at too late a stage of evolution to bring out clearly the origins. If we wish to free ourselves from the all-pervasive influence of the intellectual presumption that man in his wisdom has designed, or ever could have designed, the whole system of legal or moral rules, we should begin with a look at the primitive and even pre-human beginnings of social life.

Social theory has here much to learn from the two young sciences of ethology and cultural anthropology which in many respects have built on the foundation of social theory initially laid in the eighteenth century by the Scottish moral philosophers. In the field of law, indeed, these young disciplines go far to confirm the evolutionary teaching of Edward Coke, Matthew Hale, David Hume and Edmund Burke, F. C. von Savigny, H. S. Maine and J. C. Carter, and are wholly contrary to the rationalist constructivism of Francis Bacon or Thomas Hobbes, Jeremy Bentham or John Austin, or of the German positivists from Paul Laband to Hans Kelsen.

The lessons of ethology and cultural anthropology

The chief points on which the comparative study of behaviour has thrown such important light on the evolution of law are, first, that it has made clear that individuals had learned to observe (and enforce) rules of conduct long before such rules could be expressed in words; and second, that these rules had evolved because they led to the formation of an order of the activities of the group as a whole which, although they are the results of the regularities of the actions of the individuals, must be clearly distinguished from them, since it is the efficiency of the resulting order of actions which will determine whether groups whose members observe certain rules of conduct will prevail. [6]

In view of the fact that man became man and developed reason and language while living for something like a million years in groups held together by common rules of conduct, and that one of the first uses of reason and language must have been to teach and enforce these established rules, it will be useful first to consider the evolution of rules which were merely in fact obeyed, before we turn to the problem of their gradual articulation in words. Social orders resting on most complex systems of such rules of conduct we find even among animals very low on the evolutionary scale. For our present purposes it does not matter that on these lower evolutionary levels the rules are probably mostly innate (or transmitted genetically) and few learned (or transmitted 'culturally'). It is now well established that among the higher vertebrates learning plays an important role in transmitting such rules, so that new rules may rapidly spread among large groups and, in the case of isolated groups, produce distinct 'cultural' traditions. [7] There is little question, on the other hand, that man is also still guided not only by learned but by some innate rules. We are here chiefly interested in the learned rules and the manner of their transmission;

but in considering the problem of the interrelation of rules of conduct and the resulting overall order of actions, it does not matter with which kind of rules we have to deal, or whether, as will usually be the case, both kinds of rules interact.

The study of comparative behaviour has shown that in many animal societies the process of selective evolution has produced highly ritualized forms of behaviour governed by rules of conduct which have the effect of reducing violence and other wasteful methods of adaptation and thus secure an order of peace. This order is often based on the delimitation of territorial ranges or 'property', which serves not only to eliminate unnecessary fighting but even substitutes 'preventive' for 'repressive' checks on the growth of population, for example, through the male who has not established a territory being unable to mate and breed. Frequently we find complex orders of rank which secure that only the strongest males will propagate. Nobody who has studied the literature on animal societies will regard it as only a metaphorical expression when for instance one author speaks of 'the elaborate system of property tenure' of crayfish and the ceremonial displays through which it is maintained,[8] or when another concludes a description of the rivalry between robins by saying that 'victory does not go to the strong but to the righteous—the righteous of course being the owners of property'.[9]

We cannot give here more than these few examples of the fascinating worlds which through these studies are gradually revealed to us,[10] but must turn to the problems that arise as man, living in such groups governed by a multiplicity of rules, gradually develops reason and language and uses them to teach and enforce the rules. At this stage it is sufficient to see that rules did exist, served a function essential to the preservation of the group, and were effectively transmitted and enforced, although they had never been 'invented', expressed in words, or possessed a 'purpose' known to anyone.

Rule in this context means simply a propensity or disposition to act or not to act in a certain manner, which will manifest itself in what we call a *practice*[11] or custom. As such it will be one of the determinants of action which, however, need not show itself in every single action but may only prevail in most instances. Any such rule will always operate in combination and often in competition with other rules or dispositions and with particular impulses; and whether a rule will prevail in a particular case will depend on the strength of the propensity it describes and of the other dispositions or impulses operating at the same time. The conflict which will often arise between immediate desires and the built-in rules or inhibitions is well attested by the observation of animals. [12]

It must be particularly emphasized that these propensities or dispositions possessed by higher animals will often be of a highly general or abstract character, that is, they will be directed towards a very wide class of actions which may differ a great deal among themselves in their detail. They will in this sense certainly be much more abstract than anything incipient language can express. For the understanding of the process of gradual articulation of rules which have long been obeyed, it is important to remember that abstractions, far from being a product of language, were acquired by the mind long before it developed language. [13] The problem of the origin and function of these rules which govern both action and thought is therefore a problem wholly distinct from the problem of how they came to be articulated in verbal form. There is little doubt that even today the rules which have been thus articulated and can be communicated by language are only a part of the whole complex of rules that guide man's actions as a social being. I doubt whether anyone has yet succeeded in articulating all the rules which constitute 'fair play', for example.

The process of articulation of practices

Even the earliest deliberate efforts of headmen or chiefs of a tribe to maintain order must thus be seen as taking place inside a given framework of rules, although they were rules which existed only as a 'knowledge how' to act and not as a 'knowledge that' they could be expressed in such and such terms. Language would certainly have been used early to teach them, but only as a means of indicating the particular actions that were required or prohibited in particular situations. As in the acquisition of language itself, the individual would have to learn to act in accordance with rules by imitating particular actions corresponding to them. So long as language is not sufficiently developed to express general rules there is no other way in which rules can be taught. But although at this stage they do not exist in articulated form, they nevertheless do exist in the sense that they govern action. And those who first attempted to express them in words did not invent new rules but were endeavouring to express what they were already acquainted with. [14]

Although still an unfamiliar conception, the fact that language is often insufficient to express what the mind is fully capable of taking into account in determining action, or that we will often not be able to communicate in words what we well know how to practise, has been clearly established in many fields. [15] It is closely connected with the fact that the rules that govern action will often be much more general and abstract than anything language can yet express. Such abstract rules are learnt by imitating particular actions, from which the individual acquires 'by analogy' the capacity to act in other cases on the same principles which, however, he could never state as principles.

For our purposes this means that, not merely in the primitive tribe but also in more advanced communities, the chief or ruler will use his authority for two quite different purposes: he will do so to teach or enforce rules of conduct which he regards as established, though he may have little idea why they are important or what depends on their observance; he will also give commands for actions which seem to him necessary for the achievement of particular purposes. There will always be ranges of activities with which he will not interfere so long as the individuals observe the recognized rules, but on certain occasions, such as hunting expeditions, migrations, or warfare, his commands will have to direct the individuals to particular actions.

The different character of these two ways in which authority can be exercised would show itself even in relatively primitive conditions in the fact that in the first instance its legitimacy could be questioned while in the second it could not: the right of the chief to require particular behaviour would depend on the general recognition of a corresponding rule, while his directions to the participants of a joint enterprise would be determined by his plan for action and the particular circumstances known to him but not necessarily to the others. It would be the necessity to justify commands of the first sort which would lead to attempts to articulate the rules which they were meant to enforce. Such a necessity to express the rules in words would arise also in the case of disputes which the chief was called upon to settle. The explicit statement of the established practice or custom as a verbal rule would aim at obtaining consent about its existence and not at making a new rule; and it would rarely achieve more than an inadequate and partial expression of what was well known in practice.

The process of a gradual articulation in words of what had long been an established practice must have been a slow and complex one. [16] The first fumbling attempts to express in words what most obeyed in practice would usually not succeed in expressing only, or exhausting all of, what the individuals did in fact take into account in the determination of their actions. The unarticulated rules will therefore usually contain both more and less than what the verbal formula succeeds in expressing. On the other hand, articulation will often become necessary because the 'intuitive' knowledge may not give a clear answer to a particular question. The process of articulation will thus sometimes in effect, though not in intention, produce new rules. But the articulated rules will thereby not wholly replace the unarticulated ones, but will operate, and be intelligible, only within a framework of yet unarticulated rules.

While the process of articulation of pre-existing rules will thus often lead to alterations in the body of such rules, this will have little effect on the belief that those formulating the rules do no more, and have no power to do more, than to find and express already existing rules, a task in which fallible humans will often go wrong, but in the performance of which they have no free choice. The task will be regarded as one of discovering something which exists, not as one of creating something new, even though the result of such efforts may be the creation of something that has not existed before.

This remains true even where, as is undoubtedly often the case, those called upon to decide are driven to formulate rules on which nobody has acted before. They are concerned not only with a body of rules but also with an order of the actions resulting from the observance of these rules, which men find in an ongoing process and the preservation of which may require particular rules. The preservation of the existing order of actions towards which all the recognized rules are directed may well be seen to require some other rule for the decision of disputes for which the recognized rules supply no answer. In this sense a rule not yet existing in any sense may yet appear to be 'implicit' in the body of the existing rules, not in the sense that it is logically derivable from them, but in the sense that if the other rules are to achieve their aim, an additional rule is required.

Factual and normative rules

It is of some importance to recognize that, where we have to deal with non-articulated rules, a distinction that seems very clear and obvious with respect to articulated rules becomes much less clear and perhaps sometimes even impossible to draw. This is the distinction between descriptive rules which assert the regular recurrence of certain sequences of events (including human actions) and the normative rules which state that such sequences 'ought' to take place. It is difficult to say at what particular stage of the gradual transition from a wholly unconscious observance of such rules to their expression in articulated form this distinction becomes meaningful. Is an innate inhibition which prevents a man or animal from taking a certain action, but of which he is wholly unaware, a 'norm'? Does it become a 'norm' when an observer can see how a desire and an inhibition are in conflict, as in the case of Konrad Lorenz's wolf, whose attitude he describes by saying that 'you could see that he would like to bite his opponent's offered throat, but he just cannot'?[17] Or when it leads to a conscious conflict between a particular impulse and a feeling that 'one ought not to do it'? Or when this feeling is expressed in words ('I ought not to'), but still applied only to oneself? Or when, although not yet articulated as a verbal rule, the feeling is shared by all members of the group and leads to expressions of disapproval or even attempts at prevention and punishment when infringed? Or only when it is enforced by a recognized authority or laid down in articulated form?

It seems that the specific character usually ascribed to 'norms' which makes them belong to a different realm of discourse from statements of facts, belongs only to articulated rules, and even there only once the question is raised as to whether we ought to obey them or not. So long as such rules are merely obeyed in fact (either always or at least in most instances), and their observance is ascertainable only from actual behaviour, they do not differ from descriptive rules; they are significant as one of the determinants of action, a disposition or inhibition whose operation we infer from what we observe. If such a disposition or inhibition is produced by the teaching of an articulated rule, its effect on actual behaviour still remains a fact. To the observer the norms guiding the actions of the individuals in a group are part of the determinants of the events which he perceives and which enable him to explain the overall order of actions as he finds it.

This, of course, does not alter the circumstance that our language is so made that no valid inference can lead from a statement containing only a description of facts to a statement of what ought to be. But not all conclusions often drawn from this are compelling. It says no more than that from a statement of fact alone no statements about appropriate, desirable or expedient action, nor any decision about whether to act at all, can be derived. One can follow from the other only if at the same time some end is accepted as desirable and the argument takes the form of 'if you want this, you must do that'. But once such an assumption about the desired end is included in the premises, all sorts of normative rules may be derived from them.

To the primitive mind no clear distinction exists between the only way in which a particular result can be achieved and the way in which it ought to be achieved. Knowledge of cause and effect and knowledge of rules of conduct are still indistinguishable: there is but knowledge of *the* manner in which one must act in order to achieve any result. To the child who learns to add or multiply figures, the way in which this ought to be done is also the only way to obtain the intended result. Only when he discovers that there are other ways than those taught to him, which also will lead him to what he desires, can there arise a conflict between knowledge of fact and the rules of conduct established in the group.

A difference between all purposive action and norm-guided action exists only in so far as in the case of what we usually regard as purposive action we assume that the purpose is known to the acting person, while in the case of norm-guided action the reasons why he regards one way of acting as a possible way of achieving a desired result and another as not possible will often be unknown to him. Yet to regard one kind of action as appropriate and another as inappropriate is as much the result of a process of selection of what is effective, whether it is the consequence of the particular action producing the results desired by the individual or the consequence of action of that kind being conducive or not being conducive to the functioning of the group as a whole. The reason why all the individual members of a group do particular things in a particular way will thus often not be that only in this way they will achieve what they intend, but that only if they act in this manner will that order of the group be preserved within which their individual actions are likely to be successful. The group may have persisted only because its members have developed and transmitted ways of doing things which made the group as a whole more effective than others; but the reason why certain things are done in certain ways no member of the group needs to know.

It has, of course, never been denied that the existence of norms in a given group of men is a fact. What has been questioned is that from the circumstance that the norms are in fact obeyed the conclusion could be drawn that they ought to be obeyed. The conclusion is of course possible only if it is tacitly assumed that the continued existence of the group is desired. But if such continued existence is regarded as desirable, or even the further existence of the group as an entity with a certain order is presupposed as a fact, then it follows that certain rules of conduct (not necessarily all those which are now observed) will have to be followed by its members. [18]

Early law

It should now be easier to see why in all early civilization we find a law like that 'of the Medes and the Persians that changeth not', and why all early 'law-giving' consisted in efforts to record and make known a law that was conceived as unalterably given. A 'legislator' might endeavour to purge the law of supposed corruptions, or to restore it to its pristine purity, but it was not thought that he could make new law. The historians of law are agreed that he could make new law. The historians of law are agreed that in this respect all the famous early 'law-givers', from Ur-Nammu [19] and Hammurabi to Solon, Lykurgus and the authors of the Roman Twelve Tables, did not intend to create new law but merely to state what law was and had always been. [20]

But if nobody had the power or the intention to change the law, and only old law was regarded as good law, this does not mean that law did not continue to develop. What it means is merely that the changes which did occur were not the result of intention or design of a law-maker. To a ruler whose power rested largely on the expectation that he would enforce a law presumed to be given independently of him, this law often must have seemed more an obstacle to his efforts at deliberate organization of government than a means for his conscious purposes. It was in those activities of their subjects which they could not directly control, often mainly in the relations of these subjects with outsiders, that new rules developed outside the law enforced by the rulers, while the latter tended to become rigid precisely to the extent to which it had been articulated.

The growth of the purpose-independent rules of conduct which can produce a spontaneous order will thus often have taken place in conflict with the aims of the rulers who tended to try to turn their domain into an organization proper. It is in the *ius gentium*, the law merchant, and the practices of the ports and fairs that we must chiefly seek the steps in the evolution of law which ultimately made an open society possible. Perhaps one might even say that the development of universal rules of conduct did not begin within the organized community of the tribe but rather with the first instance of silent barter when a savage placed some offerings at the boundary of the territory of his tribe in the expectation that a return gift would be made in a similar manner, thus beginning a new custom. At any rate, it was not through direction by rulers, but through the development of customs on which expectations of the individuals could be based, that general rules of conduct came to be accepted.

The classical and the medieval tradition

Although the conception that law was the product of a deliberate human will was first fully developed in ancient Greece, its influence over the actual practice of politics remained limited. Of classical Athens at the height of its democracy we are told that 'at no time was it legal to alter the law by a simple decree of the assembly. The mover of such a decree was liable to the famous "indictment for illegal proceedings" which, if upheld by the courts, quashed the decree, and also, brought within the year, exposed the mover to heavy penalties.'[21] A change in the basic rules of just conduct, the *nomoi*, could be brought about only through a complicated procedure in which a specially elected body, the *nomothetae*, was involved. Nevertheless, we find in the Athenian democracy already the first clashes between the unfettered will of the 'sovereign' people and the tradition of the rule of law;[22] and it was chiefly because the assembly often refused to be bound by the law that Aristotle turned against this form of democracy, to which he even denied the right to be called a constitution.[23] It is in the discussions of this period that we find the first persistent efforts to draw a clear distinction between the law and the particular will of the ruler.

The law of Rome, which has influenced all Western law so profoundly, was even less the product of deliberate law-making. As all other early law it was formed at a time when 'law and the institutions of social life were considered to have always existed and nobody asked for their origin. The idea that law might be created by men is alien to the thinking of early people.'[24] It was only 'the naïve belief of later more advanced ages that all law must rest on legislation.'[25] In fact, the classical Roman civil law, on which the final compilation of Justinian was based, is almost entirely the product of law-finding by jurists and only to a very small extent the product of legislation.[26] By a process very similar to that by which later the English common law developed, and differing from it mainly in that the decisive role was played by the opinions of legal scholars (the *jurisconsults*) rather than the decisions of judges, a body of law grew up through the gradual articulation of prevailing conceptions of justice rather than by legislation.[27] It was only at the end of this development, at Byzantium rather than at Rome and under the influence of Hellenistic thinking, that the results of this process were codified under the Emperor Justinian, whose work was later falsely regarded as the model of a law created by a ruler and expressing his 'will'.

Until the rediscovery of Aristotle's *Politics* in the thirteenth century and the reception of Justinian's code in the fifteenth, however, Western Europe passed through another epoch of nearly a thousand years when law was again regarded as something given independently of human will, something to be discovered, not made, and when the conception that law could be deliberately made or altered seemed almost sacrilegious. This attitude, noticed by many earlier scholars,[28] has been given a classical description by Fritz Kern, and we can do no better than quote his main conclusions:[29]

When a case arises for which no valid law can be adduced, then the lawful men or doomsmen will make new law in the belief that what they are making is good old law, not indeed expressly handed-down, but tacitly existent. They do not, therefore, create the law: they 'discover' it. Any particular judgement in court, which we regard as a particular inference from a general established legal rule, was to the medieval mind in no way distinguishable from the legislative activity of the community; in both cases a law hidden but already existing is discovered, not created. There is, in the Middle Ages, no such thing as the 'first application of a legal rule'. Law is old; new law is a contradiction in terms; for either new law is derived explicitly or implicitly from the old, or it conflicts with the old, in which case it is not lawful. The fundamental idea remains the same;

the old law is the true law, and the true law is the old law. According to medieval ideas, therefore, the enactment of new law is not possible at all; and all legislation and legal reform is conceived of as the restoration of the good old law which has been violated.

The history of the intellectual development by which, from the thirteenth century onwards, and mainly on the European continent, law-making slowly and gradually came to be regarded as an act of the deliberate and unfettered will of the ruler, is too long and complex to be described here. From the detailed studies of this process it appears to be closely connected with the rise of absolute monarchy when the conceptions which later governed the aspirations of democracy were formed.[30] This development was accompanied by a progressive absorption of this new power of laying down new rules of just conduct into the much older power which rulers had always exercised, their power of organizing and directing the apparatus of government, until both powers became inextricably mixed up in what came to be regarded as the single power of 'legislation'.

The main resistance to this development came from the tradition of the 'law of nature'. As we have seen, the late Spanish schoolmen used the term 'natural' as a technical term to describe what had never been 'invented' or deliberately designed but had evolved in response to the necessity of the situation. But even this tradition lost its power when in the seventeenth century 'natural law' came to be understood as the design of 'natural reason'.

The only country that succeeded in preserving the tradition of the Middle Ages and built on the medieval 'liberties' the modern conception of liberty under the law was England. This was partly due to the fact that England escaped a wholesale reception of the late Roman law and with it the conception of law as the creation of some ruler; but it was probably due more to the circumstance that the common law jurists there had developed conceptions somewhat similar to those of the natural law tradition but not couched in the misleading terminology of that school. Nevertheless, 'in the sixteenth and early seventeenth century the political structure of England was not yet fundamentally different from that of the continental countries and it might still have seemed uncertain whether she would develop a highly centralized absolute monarchy as did the countries of the continent.'[31] What prevented such development was the deeply entrenched tradition of a common law that was not conceived as the product of anyone's will but rather as a barrier to all power, including that of the king—a tradition which Edward Coke was to defend against King James I and Francis Bacon, and which Matthew Hale at the end of the seventeenth century masterly restated in opposition to Thomas Hobbes. [32]

The freedom of the British which in the eighteenth century the rest of Europe came so much to admire was thus not, as the British themselves were among the first to believe and as Montesquieu later taught the world, originally a product of the separation of powers between legislature and executive, but rather a result of the fact that the law that governed the decisions of the courts was the common law, a law existing independently of anyone's will and at the same time binding upon and developed by the independent courts; a law with which parliament only rarely interfered and, when it did, mainly only to clear up doubtful points within a given body of law. One might even say that a sort of separation of powers had grown up in England, not because the 'legislature' alone made law, but because it did *not*: because the law was determined by courts independent of the power which organized and directed government, the power namely of what was misleadingly called the 'legislature'.

The distinctive attributes of law arising from custom and precedent

The important insight to which an understanding of the process of evolution of law leads is that the rules which will emerge from it will of necessity possess certain attributes which laws invented or designed by a ruler may but need not possess, and are likely to possess only if they are modelled after the kind of rules which spring from the articulation of previously existing practices. We shall only in the next chapter be able to describe fully all the characteristic properties of the law which is thus formed, and to show that it has provided the standard for what political philosophers long re-garded as *the law* in the proper meaning of the word, as contained in such expressions as the 'rule' or 'reign of law', a 'government under the law', or the 'separation of powers'. At this point we want to stress only one of the peculiar properties of this *nomos*, and will merely briefly mention the others in anticipation of later discussion. The law will consist of purpose-independent rules which govern the conduct of individuals towards each other, are intended to apply to an unknown number of further instances, and by defining a protected domain of each, enable an order of actions to form itself wherein the individuals can make feasible plans. It is usual to refer to these rules as abstract rules of conduct, and although this description is inadequate, we shall provisionally employ it for the purpose in hand. The particular point which we want to bring out here is that such law which, like the common law, emerges from the judicial process is necessarily abstract in the sense that the law created by the commands of the ruler need not be so.

The contention that a law based on precedent is more rather than less abstract than one expressed in verbal rules is so contrary to a view widely held, perhaps more among continental than among Anglo-Saxon lawyers, that it needs fuller justification. The central point can probably not be better expressed than in a famous statement by the great eighteenth-century judge Lord Mansfield, who stressed that the common law 'does not consist of particular cases, but of general principles, which are illustrated and explained by those cases'. [33] What this means is that it is part of the technique of the common law judge that from the precedents which guide him he must be able to derive rules of universal significance which can be applied to new cases.

The chief concern of a common law judge must be the expectations which the parties in a transaction would have reasonably formed on the basis of the general practices that the ongoing order of actions rests on. In deciding what expectations were reasonable in this sense he can take account only of such practices (customs or rules) as in fact could determine the expectations of the parties and such facts as may be presumed to have been known to them. And these parties would have been able to form common expectations, in a situation which in some respects must have been unique, only because they interpreted the situation in terms of what was thought to be appropriate conduct and which need not have been known to them in the form of an articulated rule.

Such rules, presumed to have guided expectations in many similar situations in the past, must be abstract in the sense of referring to a limited number of relevant circumstances and of being applicable irrespective of the particular consequences now appearing to follow from their application. By the time the judge is called upon to decide a case, the parties in the dispute will already have acted in the pursuit of their own ends and mostly in particular circumstances unknown to any authority; and the expectations which have guided their actions and in which one of them has been disappointed will have been based on what they regarded as established practices. The task of the judge will be to tell them what ought to have guided their expectations, not because anyone had told them before that this was the rule, but because this was the established custom which they ought to have known. The question for the judge here can never be whether the action in fact taken was expedient from some higher point of view, or served a particular result desired by authority, but only whether the conduct under dispute conformed to recognized rules. The only public good with which he can be concerned is the observance of those rules that the individuals could reasonably count on. He is not concerned with any ulterior purpose which somebody may have intended the rules to serve and of which he must be largely ignorant; and he will have to apply the rules even if in the particular instance the known consequences will appear to him wholly undesirable. [34] In this task he must pay no attention, as has often been emphasized by common law judges, to any wishes of a ruler or any 'reasons of state'. What must guide his decision is not any knowledge of what the whole of society requires at the particular moment, but solely what is demanded by general principles on which the going order of society is based.

It seems that the constant necessity of articulating rules in order to distinguish between the relevant and the accidental in the precedents which guide him, produces in the common law judge a capacity for discovering general principles rarely acquired by a judge who operates with a supposedly complete catalogue of applicable rules before him. When the generalizations are not supplied ready made, a capacity for formulating abstractions is apparently kept alive, which the mechanical use of verbal formulae tends to kill. The common law judge is bound to be very much aware that words are always but an imperfect expression of what his predecessors struggled to articulate.

If today the commands of a legislator often take the form of those abstract rules which have emerged from the judicial process, it is because they have been shaped after that model. But it is highly unlikely that any ruler aiming at organizing the activities of his subjects for the achievement of definite foreseeable results could ever have achieved his purpose by laying down universal rules intended to govern equally the actions of everybody. To restrain himself, as the judge does, so as to enforce only such rules, would require a degree of self-denial not to be expected from one used to issuing specific commands and to being guided in his decisions by the needs of the moment. Abstract rules are not likely to be invented by somebody concerned with obtaining particular results. It was the need to preserve an order of action which nobody had created but which was disturbed by certain kinds of behaviour that made it necessary to define those kinds of behaviour which had to be repressed.

Why grown law requires correction by legislation

The fact that all law arising out of the endeavour to articulate rules of conduct will of necessity possess some desirable properties not necessarily possessed by the commands of a legislator does not mean that in other respects such law may not develop in very undesirable directions, and that when this happens correction by deliberate legislation may not be the only practicable way out. For a variety of reasons the spontaneous process of growth may lead into an impasse from which it cannot extricate itself by its own forces or which it will at least not correct quickly enough. The development of case-law is in some respects a sort of one-way street: when it has already moved a considerable distance in one direction, it often cannot retrace its steps when some implications of earlier decisions are seen to be clearly undesirable. The fact that law that has evolved in this way has certain desirable properties does not prove that it will always be good law or even that some of its rules may not be very bad. It therefore does not mean that we can altogether dispense with legislation.[35]

There are several other reasons for this. One is that the process of judicial development of law is of necessity gradual and may prove too slow to bring about the desirable rapid adaptation of the law to wholly new circumstances. Perhaps the most important, however, is that it is not only difficult but also undesirable for judicial decisions to reverse a development, which has already taken place and is then seen to have undesirable consequences or to be downright wrong. The judge is not performing his function if he disappoints reasonable expectations created by earlier decisions. Although the judge can develop the law by deciding issues which are genuinely doubtful, he cannot really alter it, or can do so at most only very gradually where a rule has become firmly established; although he may clearly recognize that another rule would be better, or more just, it would evidently be unjust to apply it to transactions which had taken place when a different rule was regarded as valid. In such situations it is desirable that the new rule should become known before it is enforced; and this can be effected only by promulgating a new rule which is to be applied only in the future. Where a real change in the law is required, the new law can properly fulfil the proper function of all law, namely that of guiding expectations, only if it becomes known before it is applied.

The necessity of such radical changes of particular rules may be due to various causes. It may be due simply to the recognition that some past development was based on error or that it produced consequences later recognized as unjust. But the most frequent cause is probably that the development of the law has lain in the hands of members of a particular class whose traditional views made them regard as just what could not meet the more general requirements of justice. There can be do doubt that in such fields as the law on the relations between master and servant,[36] landlord and tenant, creditor and debtor, and in modern times between organized business and its customers, the rules have been shaped largely by the views of one of the parties and their particular interests—especially where, as used to be true in the first two of the instances given, it was one of the groups concerned which almost exclusively supplied the judges. This, as we shall see, does not mean that, as has been asserted, 'justice is an irrational ideal' and that 'from the point of rational cognition there are only interests of human beings and hence conflicts of interests',[37] at least when by interests we do not mean only particular aims but long-term chances which different rules offer to the different members of society. It is even less true that, as would follow from those assertions, a recognized bias of some rule in favour of a particular group can be corrected only by biasing it instead in favour of another. But such occasions when it is recognized that some hereto accepted rules are unjust in the light of more general principles of justice may well require the revision not only of single rules but of whole sections of the established system of case law. This is more than can be accomplished by decisions of particular cases in the light of existing precedents.

The origin of legislative bodies

There is no determinable point in history when the power of

deliberately changing the law in the sense in which we have been considering it was explicitly conferred on any authority. But there always existed of necessity an authority which had power to make law of a different kind, namely the rules of the organization of government, and it was to these existing makers of public law that there gradually accrued the power of changing also the rules of just conduct as the necessity of such changes became recognized. Since those rules of conduct had to be enforced by the organization of government, it seemed natural that those who determined that organization should also determine the rules it was to enforce.

A legislative power in the sense of a power of determining the rules of government existed, therefore, long before the need for a power to change the universal rules of just conduct was even recognized. Rulers faced with the task of enforcing a given law and of organizing defence and various services, had long experienced the necessity of laying down rules for their officers or subordinates, and they would have made no distinction as to whether these rules were of a purely administrative character or subsidiary to the task of enforcing justice. Yet a ruler would find it to his advantage to claim for the organizational rules the same dignity as was generally conceded to the universal rules of just conduct.

But if the laying down of such rules for the organization of government was long regarded as the 'prerogative' of its head, the need for an approval of, or a consent to, his measure by representa- tive or constituted bodies would often arise precisely because the ruler was himself supposed to be bound by the established law. And when, as in levying contributions in money or services for the purposes of government, he had to use coercion in a form not clearly prescribed by the established rules, he would have to assure himself of the support at least of his more powerful subjects. It would then often be difficult to decide whether they were merely called in to testify that this or that was established law or to approve of a particular imposition or measure thought necessary for a particular end.

It is thus misleading to conceive of early representative bodies as 'legislatures' in the sense in which the term was later employed by theorists. They were not primarily concerned with the rules of just conduct or the *nomos*. As F. W. Maitland explains:[38]

> The further back we trace our history the more impossible it is for us to draw strict lines of demarcation between the

various functions of the state: the same institution is a
legislative assembly, a governmental council, and a court of
law . . . For a long time past political theorists have insisted
on the distinction between legislation and the other functions
of government, and of course the distinction is important
though it is not always easy to draw the line with perfect
accuracy. But it seems necessary to notice that the power of
a statute is by no means confined to what a jurist or political
philosopher would consider the domain of legislation. A vast
number of statutes he would class rather as *privilegia* than as
leges; the statute lays down no general rules but deals only
with a particular case.

It was in connection with rules of the organization of government that the deliberate making of 'laws' became a familiar and
everyday procedure; every new undertaking of a government or
every change in the structure of government required some new
rules for its organization. The laying down of such new rules thus
became an accepted procedure long before anyone contemplated
using it for altering the established rules of just conduct. But when
the wish to do so arose it was almost inevitable that the task was
entrusted to the body which had always made laws in another
sense and often had also been asked to testify as to what the
established rules of just conduct were.

Allegiance and sovereignty

From the conception that legislation is the sole source of law
derive two ideas which in modern times have come to be accepted
as almost self-evident and have exercised great influence on political
developments, although they are wholly derived from that erroneous constructivism in which earlier anthropomorphic fallacies
survive. The first of these is the belief that there must be a supreme
legislator whose power cannot be limited, because this would require a still higher legislator, and so on in an infinite regress. The
other is that anything laid down by that supreme legislator is law
and only that which expresses his will is law.

The conception of the necessarily unlimited will of a supreme
legislator, which since Bacon, Hobbes and Austin has served as the
supposedly irrefutable justification of absolute power, first of
monarchs and later of democratic assemblies, appears self-evident
only if the term law is restricted to the rules guiding the deliberate

and concerted actions of an organization. Thus interpreted, law, which in the earlier sense of *nomos* was meant to be a barrier to all power, becomes instead an instrument for the use of power.

The negative answer which legal positivism gives to the question of whether there can be effective limits to the power of the supreme legislature would be convincing only if it were true that all law is always the product of the deliberate 'will' of a legislator, and that nothing could effectively limit that power except another 'will' of the same sort. The authority of a legislator always rests, however, on something which must be clearly distinguished from an act of will on a particular matter in hand, and can therefore also be limited by the source from which it derives its authority. This source is a prevailing opinion that the legislator is authorized only to prescribe what is right, where this opinion refers not to the particular content of the rule but to the general attributes which any rule of just conduct must possess. The power of the legislator thus rests on a common opinion about certain attributes which the laws he produces ought to possess, and his will can obtain the support of opinion only if its expression possesses those attributes. We shall later have to consider more fully this distinction between will and opinion. Here it must suffice to say that we shall use the term 'opinion', as distinct from an act of will on a particular matter, to describe a common tendency to approve of some particular acts of will and to disapprove of others, according to whether they do or do not possess certain attributes which those who hold a given opinion usually will not be able to specify. So long as the legislator satisfies the expectation that what he resolves will possess those attributes, he will be free so far as the particular contents of its resolutions are concerned, and will in this sense be 'sovereign'. But the allegiance on which this sovereignty rests depends on the sovereign's satisfying certain expectations concerning the general character of those rules, and will vanish when this expectation is disappointed. In this sense all power rests on, and is limited by, opinion, as was most clearly seen by David Hume. [39]

That all power rests on opinion in this sense is no less true of the powers of an absolute dictator than of those of any other authority. As dictators themselves have known best at all times, even the most powerful dictatorship crumbles if the support of opinion is withdrawn. This is the reason why dictators are so concerned to manipulate opinion through that control of information which is in their power.

The effective limitation of the powers of a legislature does therefore not require another organized authority capable of concerted action above it; it may be produced by a state of opinion which brings it about that only certain kinds of commands which the legislature issues are accepted as laws. Such opinion will be concerned not with the particular content of the decisions of the legislature but only with the general attributes of the kind of rules which the legislator is meant to proclaim and to which alone the people are willing to give support. This power of opinion does not rest on the capacity of the holders to take any course of concerted action, but is merely a negative power of withholding that support on which the power of the legislator ultimately rests.

There is no contradiction in the existence of a state of opinion which commands implicit obedience to the legislator so long as he commits himself to a general rule, but refuses obedience when he orders particular actions. And whether a particular decision of the legislator is readily recognizable as valid law need not depend solely on whether the decision has been arrived at in a prescribed manner, but may also depend on whether it consists of a universal rule of just conduct.

There is thus no logical necessity that an ultimate power must be omnipotent. In fact, what everywhere is the ultimate power, namely that opinion which produces allegiance, will be a limited power, although it in turn limits the power of all legislators. This ultimate power is thus a negative power, but as a power of withholding allegiance it limits all positive power. And in a free society in which all power rests on opinion, this ultimate power will be a power which determines nothing directly yet controls all positive power by tolerating only certain kinds of exercise of that power.

These restraints on all organized power and particularly the power of the legislator could, of course, be made more effective and more promptly operative if the criteria were explicitly stated by which it can be determined whether or not a particular decision can be a law. But the restraints which in fact have long operated on the legislatures have hardly ever been adequately expressed in words. To attempt to do so will be one of our tasks.

FIVE

NOMOS: THE LAW OF LIBERTY

As for the constitution of Crete which is described by
Ephorus, it might suffice to tell its most important provisions.
The lawgiver, he says, seems to take it for granted that liberty
is a state's highest good and for this reason alone makes
property belong specifically to those who acquire it, whereas in
condition of slavery everything belongs to the rulers and
not to the ruled.

Strabo*

The functions of the judge

We must now attempt to describe more fully the distinctive character of those rules of just conduct which emerge from the efforts
of judges to decide disputes and which have long provided the
model which legislators have tried to emulate. It has already been
pointed out that the ideal of individual liberty seems to have flourished chiefly among people where, at least for long periods, judge-
made law predominated. This we have ascribed to the circumstance
that judge-made law will of necessity possess certain attributes
which the decrees of the legislator need not possess and are likely
to possess only if the legislator takes judge-made law for his model.
In this chapter we will examine the distinct attributes of what political theorists have long regarded simply as *the law*, the lawyer's law,
or the *nomos* of the ancient Greeks and the *ius* of the Romans[1]
(and what in other European languages is distinguished as *droit*,
Recht, or *diritto* from the *loi*, *Gesetz*,[2] or *legge*), and contrast with
it in the next chapter those rules of organization of government
with which legislatures have been chiefly concerned.

The distinct character of the rules which the judge will have to
apply, and must endeavour to articulate and improve, is best
understood if we remember that he is called in to correct dis-
turbances of an order that has not been made by anyone and does

94

not rest on the individuals having been told what they must do. In most instances no authority will even have known at the time the disputed action took place what the individuals did or why they did it. The judge is in this sense an institution of a spontaneous order. He will always find such an order in existence as an attribute of an ongoing process in which the individuals are able successfully to pursue their plans because they can form expectations about the actions of their fellows which have a good chance of being met.

To appreciate the significance of this it is necessary to free ourselves wholly from the erroneous conception that there can be first a society which then gives itself laws. [3] This erroneous conception is basic to the constructivist rationalism which from Descartes and Hobbes through Rousseau and Bentham down to contemporary legal positivism has blinded students to the true relationship between law and government. It is only as a result of individuals observing certain common rules that a group of men can live together in those orderly relations which we call a society. It would therefore probably be nearer the truth if we inverted the plausible and widely held idea that law derives from authority and rather thought of all authority as deriving from law—not in the sense that the law appoints authority, but in the sense that authority commands obedience because (and so long as) it enforces a law presumed to exist independently of it and resting on a diffused opinion of what is right. Not all law can therefore be the product of legislation; but power to legislate presupposes the recognition of some common rules; and such rules which underlie the power to legislate may also limit that power. No group is likely to agree on articulated rules unless its members already hold opinions that coincide in some degree. Such coincidence of opinion will thus have to precede explicit agreement on articulated rules of just conduct, although not agreement on particular ends of action. Persons differing in their general values may occasionally agree on, and effectively collaborate for, the achievement of particular concrete purposes. But such agreement on particular ends will never suffice for forming that lasting order which we call a society.

The character of grown law stands out most clearly if we look at the condition among groups of men possessing common conceptions of justice but no common government. Groups held together by common rules, but without a deliberately created organization for the enforcement of these rules, have certainly often existed. Such a state of affairs may never have prevailed in what we would not recognize as a territorial state, but it undoubtedly often existed among such groups as merchants or persons connected by the rules of chivalry or hospitality.

Whether we ought to call 'law' the kind of rules that in these groups may be effectively enforced by opinion and by the exclusion from the group of those who break them, is a matter of terminology and therefore of convenience. [4] For our present purposes we are interested in any rules which are honoured in action and not only in rules enforced by an organization created for that purpose. It is the factual observance of the rules which is the condition for the formation of an order of actions; whether they need to be enforced or how they are enforced is of secondary interest. Factual observance of some rules no doubt preceded any deliberate enforcement. The reasons why the rules arose must therefore not be confused with the reasons which made it necessary to enforce them. Those who decided to do so may never have fully comprehended what function the rules served. But if society is to persist it will have to develop some methods of effectively teaching and often also (although this may be the same thing) of enforcing them. Yet whether they need to be enforced depends also on circumstances other than the consequences of their non-observance. So long as we are interested in the effect of the observance of the rules, it is irrelevant whether they are obeyed by the individuals because they describe the only way the individuals know of achieving certain ends, or whether some sort of pressure, or a fear of sanctions, prevents them from acting differently. The mere feeling that some action would be so outrageous that one's fellows would not tolerate it is in this context quite as significant as the enforcement by that regular procedure which we find in advanced legal systems. What is important for us at this stage is that it will always be in an effort to secure and improve a system of rules which are already observed that what we know as the apparatus of law is developed.

Such law may be gradually articulated by the endeavours of arbitrators or similar persons called in to settle disputes but who have no power of command over the actions on which they have to adjudicate. The questions which they will have to decide will not be whether the parties have obeyed anybody's will, but whether their actions have conformed to expectations which the other parties had reasonably formed because they corresponded to the practices on which the everyday conduct of the members of the group was based. The significance of customs here is that they give rise to expectations that guide people's actions, and what will be regarded as binding will therefore be those practices that everybody counts on being observed and which have thereby become the condition for the success of most activities. [5] The fulfilment of expectations which these customs secure will not be, and will not appear to be, the result of any human will, or dependent on anyone's wishes or on the particular identities of the persons involved. If a need arises to call in an impartial judge, it will be because such a person will be expected to decide the case as one of a kind which might occur anywhere and at any time, and therefore in a manner which will satisfy the expectations of any person placed in a similar position among persons not known to him individually.

How the task of the judge differs from that of the head of an organization

Even where the judge has to find rules which have never been stated and perhaps never been acted upon before, his task will thus be wholly different from that of the leader of an organization who has to decide what action ought to be taken in order to achieve particular results. It would probably never have occurred to one used to organizing men for particular actions to give his commands the form of rules equally applicable to all members of the group irrespective of their allotted tasks, if he had not already had before him the example of the judge. It therefore seems unlikely that any authority with power of command would ever have developed law in the sense in which the judges developed it, that is as rules applicable to anyone who finds himself in a position definable in abstract terms. That human intention should concern itself with laying down rules for an unknown number of future instances presupposes a feat of conscious abstraction of which primitive people are hardly capable. Abstract rules independent of any particular result aimed at were something which had to be found to prevail, not something the mind could deliberately create. If we are today so familiar with the conception of law in the sense of abstract rules that it appears obvious to us that we must also be able deliberately to make it, this is the effect of the efforts of countless generations of judges to express in words what people had learnt to observe in action. In their efforts they had to create the very language in which such rules could be expressed.

The distinctive attitude of the judge thus arises from the circumstance that he is not concerned with what any authority wants done in a particular instance, but with what private persons have 'legitimate' reasons to expect, where 'legitimate' refers to the kind of expectations on which generally his actions in that society have been based. The aim of the rules must be to facilitate that matching or tallying of the expectations on which the plans of the individuals depend for their success.

A ruler sending a judge to preserve the peace will normally not do so for the purpose of preserving an order he has created, or to see whether his commands have been carried out, but to restore an order the character of which he may not even know. Unlike a supervisor or inspector, a judge has not to see whether commands have been carried out or whether everybody has performed his assigned duties. Although he may be appointed by a higher authority, his duty will not be to enforce the will of that authority but to settle disputes that might upset an existing order; he will be concerned with particular events about which the authority knows nothing and with the actions of men who on their part had no knowledge of any particular commands of authority as to what they ought to do.

Thus, 'in its beginnings law (in the lawyer's sense) had for its end, and its sole end, to keep the peace'. [6] The rules which the judge enforces are of interest to the ruler who has sent him only so far as they preserve peace and assure that the flow of efforts of the people will continue undisturbed. They have nothing to do with what the individuals have been told to do by anybody but merely with their refraining from certain kinds of action which no one is allowed to take. They refer to certain presuppositions of an ongoing order which no one has made but which nevertheless is seen to exist.

The aim of jurisdiction is the maintenance of an ongoing order of actions

The contention that the rules which the judge finds and applies serve the maintenance of an existing order of actions implies that it is possible to distinguish between those rules and the resulting order. That they are distinct follows from the fact that only some rules of individual conduct will produce an overall order while others would make such an order impossible. What is required if the separate actions of the individuals are to result in an overall order is that they not only do not unnecessarily interfere with one another, but also that in those respects in which the success of the action of the individuals depends on some matching action by others, there will be at least a good chance that this correspondence will actually occur. But all rules can achieve in this respect is to make it easier for people to find together and to form that match; abstract rules cannot actually secure that this will always happen.

The reason why such rules will tend to develop is that the groups which happen to have adopted rules conducive to a more effective order of actions will tend to prevail over other groups with a less effective order.[7] The rules that will spread will be those governing the practice or customs existing in different groups which make some groups stronger than others. And certain rules will predominate by more successfully guiding expectations in relation to other persons who act independently. Indeed, the superiority of certain rules will become evident largely in the fact that they will create an effective order not only within a closed group but also between people who meet accidentally and do not know each other personally. They will thus, unlike commands, create an order even among people who do not pursue a common purpose. The observance of the rules by all will be important for each because the achievement of his purposes depends on it, but the respective purposes of different persons may be wholly different.

So long as the individuals act in accordance with the rules it is not necessary that they be consciously aware of the rules. It is enough that they *know how* to act in accordance with the rules without *knowing that* the rules are such and such in articulated terms. But their 'know how' will provide sure guidance only in frequently occurring situations, while in more unusual situations this intuitive certainty about what expectations are legitimate will be absent. It will be in the latter situations that there will be the necessity to appeal to men who are supposed to know more about the established rules if peace is to be preserved and quarrels to be prevented. Such a person called in to adjudicate will often find it necessary to articulate and thereby make more precise those rules about which there exist differences of opinion, and sometimes even to supply new rules where no generally recognized rules exist.

The purpose of thus articulating rules in words will in the first instance be to obtain consent to their application in a particular case. In this it will often be impossible to distinguish between the mere articulation of rules which have so far existed only as practices and the statement of rules which have never been acted upon before but which, once stated, will be accepted as reasonable by most. But in neither case will the judge be free to pronounce any rule he likes. The rules which he pronounces will have to fill a definite gap in the body of already recognized rules in a manner that will serve to maintain and improve that order of actions which the already existing rules make possible. [8]

For the understanding of the process by which such a system of rules is developed by jurisdiction it will be most instructive if we consider the situations in which a judge has not merely to apply and articulate already firmly established practices, but where there exists genuine doubt about what is required by established custom, and where in consequence the litigants may differ in good faith. In such cases where there exists a real gap in the recognized law a new rule will be likely to establish itself only if somebody is charged with the task of finding a rule which after being stated is recognized as appropriate.

Thus, although rules of just conduct, like the order of actions they make possible, will in the first instance be the product of spontaneous growth, their gradual perfection will require the deliberate efforts of judges (or others learned in the law) who will improve the existing system by laying down new rules. Indeed, law as we know it could never have fully developed without such efforts of judges, or even the occasional intervention of a legislator to extricate it from the dead ends into which the gradual evolution may lead it, or to deal with altogether new problems. Yet it remains still true that the system of rules as a whole does not owe its structure to the design of either judges or legislators. It is the outcome of a process of evolution in the course of which spontaneous growth of customs and deliberate improvements of the particulars of an existing system have constantly interacted. Each of these two factors has had to operate, within the conditions the other has contributed, to assist in the formation of a factual order of actions, the particular content of which will always depend also on circumstances other than the rules of law. No system of law has ever been designed as a whole, and even the various attempts at codification could do no more than systematize an existing body of law and in doing so supplement it or eliminate inconsistencies.

The judge will thus often have to solve a puzzle to which there may indeed be more than one solution, but in most instances it will be difficult enough to find even one solution which fits all the conditions it must satisfy. The judge's task will thus be an intellectual task, not one in which his emotions or personal preferences, his sympathy with the plight of one of the contestants or his opinion of the importance of the particular objective, may affect his decision. There will be given to him a definite aim, although not a particular concrete end, namely the aim of improving a given order of actions by laying down a rule that would prevent the recurrence of such conflicts as have occurred. In endeavouring to perform this task he will always have to move in a given cosmos of rules which he must accept and will have to fit into this cosmos a piece required by the aim which the system as a whole serves.

'Actions towards others' and the protection of expectations

Since for a case to come before a judge a dispute must have arisen, and since judges are not normally concerned with relations of command and obedience, only such actions of individuals as affect other persons, or, as they are traditionally described, actions towards other persons (*operationes quae sunt ad alterum*[9]) will give rise to the formulation of legal rules. We shall presently have to examine the difficult question of how such 'actions towards others' are to be defined. At the moment we want merely to point out that actions which are clearly not of this kind, such as what a person does alone within his four walls, or even the voluntary collaboration of several persons, in a manner which clearly cannot affect or harm others, can never become the subject of rules of conduct that will concern a judge. This is important because it answers a problem that has often worried students of these matters, namely that even rules which are perfectly general and abstract might still be serious and unnecessary restrictions of individual liberty.[10] Indeed, such general rules as those requiring religious conformity may well be felt to be the most severe infringement of personal liberty. Yet the fact is simply that such rules are not rules limiting conduct towards others or, as we shall define these, rules delimiting a protected domain of individuals. At least where it is not believed that the whole group may be punished by a supernatural power for the sins of individuals, there can arise no such rules from the limitation of conduct towards others, and therefore from the settlements of disputes.[11]

But what are 'actions towards others', and to what extent can conflict between them be prevented by rules of conduct? The law evidently cannot prohibit all actions which may harm others, not only because no one can foresee all the effects of any action, but also because most changes of plans which new circumstances suggest to some are likely to be to the disadvantage of some others. The protection against disappointment of expectation which the law can give in an ever changing society will always be only the protection of some expectations but not of all. And some harm knowingly caused to others is even essential for the preservation of a spontaneous order: the law does not prohibit the setting up of a new business even if this is done in the expectation that it will lead to the failure of another. The task of rules of just conduct can thus only be to tell people which expectations they can count on and which not.

The development of such rules will evidently involve a continuous interaction between the rules of law and expectations: while new rules will be laid down to protect existing expectations, every new rule will also tend to create new expectation. [12] As some of the prevailing expectations will always conflict with each other, the judge will constantly have to decide which is to be treated as legitimate and in doing so will provide the basis for new expectations. This will in some measure always be an experimental process, since the judge (and the same applies to the law-maker) will never be able to foresee all the consequences of the rule he lays down, and will often fail in his endeavour to reduce the sources of conflicts of expectations. Any new rule intended to settle one conflict may well prove to give rise to new conflicts at another point, because the establishment of a new rule always acts on an order of actions that the law alone does not wholly determine. Yet it is only by their effects on that order of actions, effects which will be discovered only by trial and error, that the adequacy or inadequacy of the rules can be judged.

In a dynamic order of actions only some expectations can be protected

In the course of this process it will be found not only that not all expectations can be protected by general rules, but even that the chance of as many expectations as possible being fulfilled will be most enhanced if some expectations are systematically disappointed. This means also that it is not possible or desirable to prevent all actions which will harm others but only certain kinds of actions. It is regarded as fully legitimate to switch patronage and thereby disappoint the confident expectations of those with whom one used to deal. The harm that one does to another which the law aims to prevent is thus not all harm but only the disappointment of such expectations as the law designates as legitimate. Only in this way can 'do not harm others' be made a rule with meaningful content for a group of men who are allowed to pursue their own aims on the basis of their own knowledge. What can be secured to each is not that no other person will interfere with the pursuit of his aims, but only that he will not be interfered with in the use of certain means.

In an external environment which constantly changes and in which consequently some individuals will always be discovering new facts, and where we want them to make use of this new knowledge, it is clearly impossible to protect all expectations. It would decrease rather than increase certainty if the individuals were prevented from adjusting their plans of action to new facts whenever they became known to them. In fact, many of our expectations can be fulfilled only because others constantly alter their plans in the light of new knowledge. If all our expectations concerning the actions of particular other persons were protected, all those adjustments to which we owe it that in constantly changing circumstances somebody can provide for us what we expect would be prevented. Which expectations ought to be protected must therefore depend on how we can maximize the fulfilment of expectations as a whole.

Such maximization would certainly not be achieved by requiring the individuals to go on doing what they have been doing before. In a world in which some of the facts are unavoidably uncertain, we can achieve some degree of stability and therefore predictability of the overall result of the activities of all only if we allow each to adapt himself to what he learns in a manner which must be unforeseeable to others. It will be through such constant change in the particulars that an abstract overall order will be maintained in which we are able from what we see to draw fairly reliable inferences as to what to expect.

We have merely for a moment to consider the consequences that would follow if each person were required to continue to do what the others had learned to expect from him in order to see that this would rapidly lead to a breakdown of the whole order. If the individuals endeavoured to obey such instructions, some would at once find it physically impossible to do so because some of the circumstances had changed. But the effects of their failing to meet expectations would in turn place others in a similar position, and these effects would extend to an ever increasing circle of persons. (This, incidentally, is one of the reasons why a completely planned system is apt to break down.) Maintaining the overall flow of results in a complex system of production requires great elasticity of the actions of the elements of that system, and it will only be through unforeseeable changes in the particulars that a high degree of predictability of the overall results can be achieved.

We shall later (in volume 2, chapter 10) have to consider more fully the apparent paradox that in the market it is through the systematic disappointment of some expectations that on the whole expectations are as effectively met as they are. This is the manner in which the principle of 'negative feedback' operates. At the moment it should merely be added, to prevent a possible misunderstanding, that the fact that the overall order shows greater regularity than the individual facts has nothing to do with those probabilities which may result from the random movement of elements with which statistics deals, for the individual actions are the product of a systematic mutual adjustment.

Our immediate concern is to bring out that this order of actions based on certain expectations will to some extent always have existed as a fact before people would endeavour to ensure that their expectations would be fulfilled. The existing order of actions will in the first instance simply be a fact which men count on and will become a value which they are anxious to preserve only as they discover how dependent they are on it for the successful pursuit of their aims. We prefer to call it a value rather than an end because it will be a condition which all will want to preserve although no one has aimed at deliberately producing it. Indeed, although all will be aware that their chances depend on the preservation of an order, none would probably be able to describe the character of that order. This will be so because the order cannot be defined in terms of any particular observable facts but only in terms of a system of abstract relationships that will be preserved through the changes of the particulars. It will be, as we have said before, not something visible or otherwise perceptible but something which can only be mentally reconstructed.

Yet, although the order may appear to consist simply in the obedience to rules, and it is true that the obedience to rules is needed to secure order, we have also seen that not all rules will secure order. Whether the established rules will lead to the formation of an overall order in any given set of circumstances will rather depend on their particular content. The obedience to unsuitable rules may well become the cause of disorder, and there are some conceivable rules of individual conduct which clearly would make impossible the integration of individual actions into an overall order.

The 'values' which the rules of just conduct serve will thus not be particulars but abstract features of an existing factual order which men will wish to enhance because they have found them to be conditions of the effective pursuit of a multiplicity of various, divergent, and unpredictable purposes. The rules aim at securing certain abstract characteristics of the overall order of our society that we would like it to possess to a higher degree. We endeavour to make it prevail by improving the rules which we first find underlying current actions. These rules, in other words, are first the property of a factual state of affairs which no one has deliberately created and which therefore has had no purpose, but which, after we begin to understand its importance for the successful pursuit of all our actions, we may try to improve.

While it is, of course, true that norms cannot be derived from premises that contain only facts, this does not mean that the acceptance of some norms aiming at certain kinds of results may not in certain factual circumstances oblige us to accept other norms, simply because in these circumstances the accepted norms will serve the ends which are their justification only if certain other norms are also obeyed. Thus, if we accept a given system of norms without question and discover that in a certain factual situation it does not achieve the result it aims at without some complementary rules, these complementary rules will be required by those already established, although they are not logically entailed by them. And since the existence of such other rules is usually tacitly presumed, it is at least not wholly false, though not quite exact, to contend that the appearance of some new facts may make certain new norms necessary.

An important consequence of this relation between the system of rules of conduct and the factual order of actions is that there can never be a science of law that is purely a science of norms and takes no account of the factual order at which it aims. Whether a new norm fits into an existing system of norms will not be a problem solely of logic, but will usually be a problem of whether, in the existing factual circumstances, the new norm will lead to an order of compatible actions. This follows from the fact that abstract rules of conduct determine particular actions only together with particular circumstances. The test of whether a new norm fits into the existing system may thus be a factual one; and a new norm that logically may seem to be wholly consistent with the already recognized ones may yet prove to be in conflict with them if in some set of circumstances it allows actions which will clash with others permitted by the existing norms. This is the reason why the Cartesian or 'geometric' treatment of law as a pure 'science of norms', where all rules of law are deduced from explicit premises, is so misleading. We shall see that it must fail even in its immediate aim of making judicial decisions more predictable. Norms cannot be judged according to whether they fit with other norms in isolation from facts, because whether the actions which they permit are mutually compatible or not depends on facts.

This is the basic insight which through the history of jurisprudence has constantly appeared in the form of a reference to the 'nature of things' (the *natura rerum* or *Natur der Sache*), [13] which we find in the often quoted statement of O. W. Holmes, that 'the life of law has not been logic, it has been experience', [14] or in such various expressions as 'the exigencies of social life', [15] the 'compatibility' [16] or the 'reconcilability' [17] of the actions to which the law refers.

The maximal coincidence of expectations is achieved by the delimitation of protected domains

The main reason why it is so difficult to see that rules of conduct serve to enhance the certainty of expectations is that they do so not by determining a particular concrete state of things, but by determining only an abstract order which enables its members to derive from the particulars known to them expectations that have a good chance of being correct. This is all that can be achieved in a world where some of the facts change in an unpredictable manner and where order is achieved by the individuals adjusting themselves to new facts whenever they become aware of them. What can remain constant in such an overall order which continually adjusts itself to external changes, and provides the basis of predictions, can only be a system of abstract relationships and not its particular elements. This means that every change must disappoint some expectations, but that this very change which disappoints some expectations creates a situation in which again the chance to form concrete expectations is as great as possible.

Such a condition can evidently be achieved only by protecting some and not all expectations, and the central problem is which expectations must be assured in order to maximize the possibility of expectations in general being fulfilled. This implies a distinction between such 'legitimate' expectations which the law must protect and others which it must allow to be disappointed. And the only method yet discovered of defining a range of expectations which will be thus protected, and thereby reducing the mutual interference of people's actions with each other's intentions, is to demarcate for every individual a range of permitted actions by designating (or rather making recognizable by the application of rules to the concrete facts) ranges of objects over which only particular individuals are allowed to dispose and from the control of which all others are excluded. The range of actions in which each will be secured against the interference of others can be determined by rules equally applicable to all only if these rules make it possible to ascertain which particular objects each may command for his purposes. In other words, rules are required which make it possible at each moment to ascertain the boundary of the protected domain of each and thus to distinguish between the *meum* and the *tuum*.

The understanding that 'good fences make good neighbours',[18] that is, that men can use their own knowledge in the pursuit of their own ends without colliding with each other only if clear boundaries can be drawn between their respective domains of free action, is the basis on which all known civilization has grown. Property, in the wide sense in which it is used to include not only material things, but (as John Locke defined it) the 'life, liberty and estates' of every individual, is the only solution men have yet discovered to the problem of reconciling individual freedom with the absence of conflict. Law, liberty, and property are an inseparable trinity. There can be no law in the sense of universal rules of conduct which does not determine boundaries of the domains of freedom by laying down rules that enable each to ascertain where he is free to act.

This was long regarded as self-evident and needing no proof. It was, as the quotation placed at the head of this chapter shows, as clearly understood by the ancient Greeks as by all founders of liberal political thought, from Milton[19] and Hobbes[20] through Montesquieu[21] to Bentham[22] and re-emphasized more recently by H. S. Maine[23] and Lord Acton.[24] It has been challenged only in comparatively recent times by the constructivist approach of socialism and under the influence of the erroneous idea that property had at some late stage been 'invented' and that before that there had existed an earlier state of primitive communism. This myth has been completely refuted by anthropological research.[25] There can be no question now that the recognition of property preceded the rise of even the most primitive cultures, and that certainly all that we call civilization has grown up on the basis of that spontaneous order of actions which is made possible by the delimitation of protected domains of individuals or groups. Although the socialist thinking of our time has succeeded in bringing this insight under the suspicion of being ideologically inspired, it is as well demonstrated a scientific truth as any we have attained in this field.

Before we proceed further it is necessary to guard ourselves against a common misunderstanding about the relations of the rules of law and the property of particular individuals. The classical formula that the aim of rules of just conduct is to assign to each his due (*suum cuique tribuere*) is often interpreted to mean that the law by itself assigns to particular individuals particular things. It does nothing of the kind, of course. It merely provides rules by which it is possible to ascertain from particular facts to whom particular things belong. The concern of the law is not who the particular persons shall be to whom particular things belong, but merely to make it possible to ascertain boundaries which have been determined by the actions of individuals within the limits drawn by those rules, but determined in their particular contents by many other circumstances. Nor must the classical formula be interpreted, as it sometimes is, as referring to what is called 'distributive justice', or as aiming at a state or a distribution of things which, apart from the question of how it has been brought about, can be described as just or unjust. The aim of the rules of law is merely to prevent as much as possible, by drawing boundaries, the actions of different individuals from interfering with each other; they cannot alone determine, and also therefore cannot be concerned with, what the result for different individuals will be.

It is only through thus defining the protected sphere of each that the law determines what are those 'actions towards others' which it regulates, and that its general prohibition of actions 'harming others' is given a determinable meaning. The maximal certainty of expectations which can be achieved in a society in which individuals are allowed to use their knowledge of constantly changing circumstances for their equally changing purposes is secured by rules which tell everyone which of these circumstances must not be altered by others and which he himself must not alter.

Precisely where those boundaries are most effectively drawn is a very difficult question to which we certainly have not yet found all the final answers. The conception of property certainly did not fall ready made from heaven. Nor have we yet succeeded everywhere in so delimiting the individual domain as to constrain the owner in his decisions to take account of all those effects (and only of those effects) we could wish. In our efforts to improve the principles of demarcation we cannot but build on an established system of rules which serves as the basis of the going order maintained by the institution of property. Because the drawing of boundaries serves a function which we are beginning to understand, it is meaningful to ask whether in particular instances the boundary has been drawn in the right place, or whether in view of changed conditions an established rule is still adequate. Where the boundary ought to be drawn, however, will usually not be a decision which can be made arbitrarily. If new problems arise as a result of changes in circumstances and raise, for example, problems of demarcation, where in the past the question as to who had a certain right was irrelevant, and the right in consequence was neither claimed nor assigned, the task will be to find a solution which serves the same general aim as the other rules which we take for granted. The rationale of the existing system may for instance clearly require that electric power be included in the concept of property, though established rules may confine it to tangible objects. Sometimes, as in the case of electro-magnetic waves, no sort of spatial boundaries will provide a working solution and altogether new conceptions of how to allocate control over such things may have to be found. Only where, as in the case of moveable objects (the 'chattels' of the law), it was approximately true that the effects of what the owner did with his property in general affected only him and nobody else, could ownership include the right to use or abuse the object in any manner he liked. But only where both the benefit and the harm caused by the particular use were confined to the domain in which the owner was interested did the conception of exclusive control provide a sufficient answer to the problem. The situation is very different as soon as we turn from chattels to real estate, where the 'neighbourhood effects' and the like make the problem of drawing appropriate 'boundaries' much more difficult.

We shall in a later context have to consider certain further consequences which follow from these considerations, such as that the rules of just conduct are essentially negative in that they aim only at preventing injustice, and that they will be developed by the consistent application to the inherited body of law of the equally negative test of compatibility; and that by the persistent application of this test we can hope to approach justice without ever finally realizing it. We shall then have to return to this complex of questions not from the angle of the properties which judge-made law necessarily possesses, but from the angle of the properties which the law of liberty ought to possess and which therefore should be observed in the process of deliberate law-making.

We must also leave to a later chapter the demonstration that what is called the maximization of the available aggregate of goods and services is an incidental though highly desirable by-product of that matching of expectations which is all the law can aim to facilitate. We shall then see that only by aiming at a state in which a mutual correspondence of expectations is likely to come about can the law help to produce that order resting on an extensive and spontaneous division of labour to which we owe our material wealth.

The general problem of the effects of values on facts

We have repeatedly emphasized that the importance of the rules of just conduct is due to the fact that the observance of these values leads to the formation of certain complex factual structures, and that in this sense important facts are dependent on the prevalence of values which are not held because of an awareness of these factual consequences. Since this relationship is rarely appreciated, some further remarks about its significance will be in place.

What is frequently overlooked is that the facts which result from certain values being held are not those to which the values which guide the actions of the several individuals are attached, but a pattern comprising the actions of many individuals, a pattern of which the acting individuals may not even be aware of and which was certainly not the aim of their actions. But the preservation of this emerging order or pattern which nobody has aimed at but whose existence will come to be recognized as the condition for the successful pursuit of many other aims will in turn also be regarded as a value. This order will be defined not by the rules governing individual conduct but by the matching of expectations which the observance of the rules will produce. But if such a factual state comes to be regarded as a value, it will mean that this value can be achieved only if people are guided in their actions by other values (the rules of conduct) which to them, since they are not aware of their functions, must appear as ultimate values. The resulting order is thus a value which is the unintended and unknown result of the observance of other values.

One consequence of this is that different prevailing values may sometimes be in conflict with each other, or that an accepted value may require the acceptance of another value, not because of any logical relation between them, but through facts which are not their object but the unintended consequences of their being honoured in action. We shall thus often find several different values which become interdependent through the factual conditions that they produce, although the acting persons may not be aware of such an interdependence in the sense that we can obtain the one only if we observe the other. Thus, what we regard as civilization may depend on the factual condition that the several plans of action of different individuals become so adjusted to each other that they can be carried out in most cases; and this condition in turn will be achieved only if the individuals accept private property as a value. Connections of this kind are not likely to be understood until we have learnt to distinguish clearly between the regularities of individual conduct which are defined by rules and the overall order which will result from the observance of certain kinds of rules.

The understanding of the role which values play here is often prevented by substituting for 'values' factual terms like 'habits' or 'practices'. It is, however, not possible in the account of the formation of an overall order to replace adequately the conception of values which guide individual action with a statement of the observed regularities in the behaviour of individuals, because we are not in fact able to reduce exhaustively the values that guide action to a list of observable actions. Conduct guided by a value is recognizable by us only because we are acquainted with that value. 'The habit of respecting another's property', for example, can be observed only if we know the rules of property, and though we may reconstruct the latter from the observed behaviour, the reconstruction will always contain more than a description of particular behaviour.

The complex relationship between values and facts creates certain familiar difficulties for the social scientist who studies complex social structures that exist only because the individuals composing them hold certain values. In so far as he takes for granted the overall structure which he studies, he also implicitly presupposes that the values on which it is based will continue to be held. This may be without significance when he studies a society other than his own, as is the case with the social anthropologist who neither wishes to influence the members of the society he studies nor expects that they will take notice of what he says. But the situation is different for the social scientist who is asked for advice on how to reach particular goals within a given society. In any suggestion for modification or improvement of such an order he will have to accept the values which are indispensable for its existence, as it would clearly be inconsistent to try to improve some particular aspect of the order and at the same time propose means that would destroy the values on which the whole order rests. He will have to argue on premises which contain values, and there is no logical flaw if in arguing from such premises he arrives at conclusions which also contain values.

The 'purpose' of law

The insight that the law serves, or is the necessary condition for, the formation of a spontaneous order of actions, though vaguely present in much of legal philosophy, is thus a conception which has been difficult to formulate precisely without the explanation of that order provided by social theory, particularly economics. The idea that the law 'aimed' at some sort of factual circumstance, or that some state of facts would emerge only if some rules of conduct were generally obeyed, we find expressed early, especially in the late schoolmen's conception of law as being determined by the 'nature of things'. It is, as we have already mentioned, at the bottom of the insistence on the law being an 'empirical' or 'experimental' science. But to conceive as a goal an abstract order, the particular manifestation of which no one could predict, and which was determined by properties no one could precisely define, was too much at variance with what most people regarded as an appropriate goal of rational action. The preservation of an enduring system of abstract relationships, or of the order of a cosmos with constantly changing content, did not fit into what men ordinarily understood by a purpose, goal or end of deliberate action.

We have already seen that in the usual sense of purpose, namely the anticipation of a particular, foreseeable event, the law indeed does not serve any purpose but countless different purposes of different individuals. It provides only the means for a large number of different purposes that as a whole are not known to anybody. In the ordinary sense of purpose law is therefore not a means to any purpose, but merely a condition for the successful pursuit of most purposes. Of all multi-purpose instruments it is probably the one after language which assists the greatest variety of human purposes. It certainly has not been made for any one known purpose but rather has developed because it made people who operated under it more effective in the pursuit of their purposes.

Although people are usually well enough aware that in some sense the rules of law are required to preserve 'order', they tend to identify this order with obedience to the rules and will not be aware that the rules serve an order in a different way, namely to effect a certain correspondence between the action of different persons.

These two different conceptions of the 'purpose' of law show themselves clearly in the history of legal philosophy. From Immanuel Kant's emphasis on the 'purposeless' character of the rules of just conduct,[26] to the Utilitarians from Bentham to Ihering who regard purpose as the central feature of law, the ambiguity of the concept of purpose has been a constant source of confusion. If 'purpose' refers to concrete foreseeable results of particular actions, the particularistic utilitarianism of Bentham is certainly wrong. But if we include in 'purpose' the aiming at conditions which will assist the formation of an abstract order, the particular contents of which are unpredictable, Kant's denial of purpose is justified only so far as the application of a rule to a particular instance is concerned, but certainly not for the system of rules as a whole. From such confusion David Hume's stress on the function of the system of law as a whole irrespective of the particular effects ought to have protected later writers. The central insight is wholly contained in Hume's emphasis on the fact that 'the benefit . . . arises from the whole scheme or system . . . only from the observance of the general rule . . . without taking into consideration . . . any particular consequences which may result from the determination of these laws, in any particular case which offers.'[27]

Only when it is clearly recognized that the order of actions is a factual state of affairs distinct from the rules which contribute to its formation can it be understood that such *an abstract order can be the aim of the rules of conduct.* The understanding of this relationship is therefore a necessary condition for the understanding of law. But the task of explaining this causal relationship has in modern times been left to a discipline that had become wholly separate from the study of law and was generally as little understood by the lawyers as the law was understood by the students of economic theory. The demonstration by the economists that the market produced a spontaneous order was regarded by most lawyers with distrust or even as a myth. Although its existence is today recognized by socialist economists as well as by all others, the resistance of most constructivist rationalists to admitting the existence of such an order still blinds most persons who are not professional economists to the insight which is fundamental to all understanding of the relation between law and the order of human actions. Without such an insight into what the scoffers still deride as the 'invisible hand', the function of rules of just conduct is indeed unintelligible, and lawyers rarely possess it. Fortunately it is not necessary for the performance of their everyday task. Only in the philosophy of law, in so far as it guides jurisdiction and legislation, has the lack of such a comprehension of the function of law become significant. It has resulted in a frequent interpretation of law as an instrument of organization for particular purposes, an interpretation which is of course true enough of one kind of law, namely public law, but wholly inappropriate with regard to the *nomos* or lawyer's law. And the predominance of this interpretation has become one of the chief causes of the progressive transformation of the spontaneous order of a free society into the organization of a totalitarian order.

This unfortunate situation has in no way been remedied by the modern alliance of law with sociology which, unlike economics, has become very popular with some lawyers. For the effect of the alliance has been to direct the attention of the lawyer to the specific effects of particular measures rather than to the connection between the rules of law and the overall order. It is not in the descriptive branches of sociology but only in the theory of the overall order of society that an understanding of the relations between law and social order can be found. And because science seems to have been understood by the lawyers to mean the ascertainment of particular facts rather then an understanding of the overall order of society, the ever repeated pleas for co-operation between law and the social sciences have so far not borne much fruit. While it is easy enough to pick from descriptive sociological studies knowledge of some particular facts, the comprehension of that overall order which the rules of just conduct serve requires the mastery of a complex theory which cannot be acquired in a day. Social science conceived as a body of inductive generalizations drawn from the observation of limited groups, such as most empirical sociology undertakes, has indeed little to contribute to an understanding of the function of law.

This is not to suggest that the overall order of society which the rules of just conduct serve is exclusively a matter of economics. But so far only economics has developed a theoretical technique suitable for dealing with such spontaneous abstract orders, which is only now slowly and gradually being applied to orders other than the market. The market order is probably also the only comprehensive order extending over the whole field of human society. It must at any rate be the only one we can fully consider in this book.

The articulation of the law and the predictability of judicial decisions

The order that the judge is expected to maintain is thus not a particular state of things but the regularity of a process which rests on some of the expectations of the acting persons being protected from interference by others. He will be expected to decide in a manner which in general will correspond to what the people regard as just, but he may sometimes have to decide that what *prima facie* appears to be just may not be so because it disappoints legitimate expectations. Here he will have to draw his conclusions not exclusively from articulated premises but from a sort of 'situational logic', based on the requirements of an existing order of actions which is at the same time the undesigned result and the rationale of all those rules which he must take for granted. While the judge's starting point will be the expectations based on already established rules, he will often have to decide which of conflicting expectations held in equally good faith and equally sanctioned by recognized rules is to be regarded as legitimate. Experience will often prove that in new situations rules which have come to be accepted lead to conflicting expectations. Yet although in such situations there will be no known rule to guide him, the judge will still not be free to decide in any manner he likes. If the decision cannot be logically deduced from recognized rules, it still must be consistent with the existing body of such rules in the sense that it serves the same order of actions as these rules. If the judge finds that a rule counted on by a litigant in forming his expectations is false even though it may be widely accepted and might even be universally approved if stated, this will be because he discovers that in some circumstances it clashes with expectations based on other rules. 'We all thought this to be a just rule, but now it proves to be unjust' is a meaningful statement, describing an experience in which it becomes apparent that our conception of the justice or injustice of a particular rule is not simply a matter of 'opinion' or 'feeling', but depends on the requirements of an existing order to which we are committed—an order which in new situations can be maintained only if one of the old rules is modified or a new rule is added. The reason why in such a situation either or even both of the rules counted on by the litigants will have to be modified will not be that their application in the particular case would cause hardship, or that any other consequence in the particular instance would be undesirable, but that the rules have proved insufficient to prevent conflicts.

If the judge here were confined to decisions which could be logically deduced from the body of already articulated rules, he would often not be able to decide a case in a manner appropriate to the function which the whole system of rules serves. This throws important light on a much discussed issue, the supposed greater certainly of the law under a system in which all rules of law have been laid down in written or codified form, and in which the judge is restricted to applying such rules as have become written law. The whole movement for codification has been guided by the belief that it increases the predictability of judicial decisions. In my own case even the experience of thirty odd years in the common law world was not enough to correct this deeply rooted prejudice, and only my return to a civil law atmosphere has led me seriously to question it. Although legislation can certainly increase the certainty of the law on particular points, I am now persuaded that this advantage is more than offset if its recognition leads to the requirement that *only* what has thus been expressed in statutes should have the force of law. It seems to me that judicial decisions may in fact be more predictable if the judge is also bound by generally held views of what is just, even when they are not supported by the letter of the law, than when he is restricted to deriving his decisions only from those among accepted beliefs which have found expression in the written law.

That the judge can, or ought to, arrive at his decisions exclusively by a process of logical inference from explicit premises always has been and must be a fiction. For in fact the judge never proceeds in this way. As has been truly said, 'the trained intuition of the judge continuously leads him to right results for which he is puzzled to give unimpeachable legal reasons'. [28] The other view is a characteristic product of the constructivist rationalism which regards all rules as deliberately made and therefore capable of exhaustive statement. It appears, significantly, only in the eighteenth century and in connection with criminal law [29] where the legitimate desire to restrict the power of the judge to the application of what was unquestionably stated as law was dominant. But even the formula *nulla poena sine lege*, in which C. Beccaria expressed this idea, is not necessarily part of the rule of law if by 'law' is meant only written rules promulgated by the legislator, and not any rules whose binding character would at once be generally recognized if they were expressed in words. Characteristically English common law has never recognized the principle in the first sense, [30] even though it always accepted it in the second. Here the old conviction that a rule may exist which everybody is assumed to be capable of observing, although it has never been articulated as a verbal statement, has persisted to the present day as part of the law.

Whatever one may feel, however, about the desirability of tying the judge to the application of the written law in criminal matters, where the aim is essentially to protect the accused and let the guilty escape rather than punish the innocent, there is little case for it where the judge must aim at equal justice between litigants. Here the requirement that he must derive his decision exclusively from the written law and at most fill in obvious gaps by resort to unwritten principles would seem to make the certainty of the law rather less than greater. It seems to me that in most instances in which judicial decisions have shocked public opinion and have run counter to general expectations, this was because the judge felt that he had to stick to the letter of the written law and dared not depart from the result of the syllogism in which only explicit statements of that law could serve as premises. Logical deduction from a limited number of articulated premises always means following the 'letter' rather than the 'spirit' of the law. But the belief that everyone must be able to foresee the consequences that will follow in an unforeseen factual situation from an application of those statements of the already articulated basic principles is clearly an illusion. It is now probably universally admitted that no code of law can be without gaps. The conclusion to be derived from this would seem to be not merely that the judge must fill in such gaps by appeal to yet unarticulated principles, but also that, even when those rules which have been articulated seem to give an unambiguous answer, if they are in conflict with the general sense of justice he should be free to modify his conclusions when he can find some unwritten rule which justifies such modification and which, when articulated, is likely to receive general assent.

In this connection even John Locke's contention that in a free society all law must be 'promulgated' or 'announced' beforehand would seem to be a product of the constructivist idea of all law as being deliberately made. It is erroneous in the implication that by confining the judge to the application of already articulated rules we will increase the predictability of his decisions. What has been promulgated or announced beforehand will often be only a very imperfect formulation of principles which people can better honour in action than express in words. Only if one believes that all law is an expression of the will of a legislator and has been invented by him, rather than an expression of the principles required by the exigencies of a going order, does it seem that previous announcement is an indispensable condition of knowledge of the law. Indeed it is likely that few endeavours by judges to improve the law have come to be accepted by others unless they found expressed in them what in a sense they 'knew' already.

The function of the judge is confined to a spontaneous order

The contention that the judges by their decisions of particular cases gradually approach a system of rules of conduct which is most conducive to producing an efficient order of actions becomes more plausible when it is realized that this is in fact merely the same kind of process as that by which all intellectual evolution proceeds. As in all other fields advance is here achieved by our moving within an existing system of thought and endeavouring by a process of piecemeal tinkering, or 'immanent criticism', to make the whole more consistent both internally as well as with the facts to which the rules are applied. Such 'immanent criticism' is the main instrument of the evolution of thought, and an understanding of this process the characteristic aim of an evolutionary (or critical) as distinguished from the constructivist (or naïve) rationalism.

The judge, in other words, serves, or tries to maintain and improve, a going order which nobody has designed, an order that has formed itself without the knowledge and often against the will of authority, that extends beyond the range of deliberate organization on the part of anybody, and that is not based on the individuals doing anybody's will, but on their expectations becoming mutually adjusted. The reason why the judge will be asked to intervene will be that the rules which secure such a matching of expectations are not always observed, or clear enough, or adequate to prevent conflicts even if observed. Since new situations in which the established rules are not adequate will constantly arise, the task of preventing conflict and enhancing the compatibility of actions by appropriately delimiting the range of permitted actions is of necessity a never-ending one, requiring not only the application of already established rules but also the formulation of new rules necessary for the preservation of the order of actions. In their endeavour to cope with new problems by the application of 'principles' which they have to distil from the *ratio decidendi* of earlier decisions, and so to develop these inchoate rules (which is what 'principles' are) that they will produce the desired effect in new situations, neither the judges nor the parties involved need to know anything about the nature of the resulting overall order, or about any 'interest of society' which they serve, beyond the fact that the rules are meant to assist the individuals in successfully forming expectations in a wide range of circumstances.

The efforts of the judge are thus part of that process of adaptation of society to circumstances by which the spontaneous order grows. He assists in the process of selection by upholding those rules which, like those which have worked well in the past, make it more likely that expectations will match and not conflict. He thus becomes an organ of that order. But even when in the performance of this function he creates new rules, he is not a creator of a new order but a servant endeavouring to maintain and improve the functioning of an existing order. And the outcome of his efforts will be a characteristic instance of those 'products of human action but not of human design' in which the experience gained by the experimentation of generations embodies more knowledge than was possessed by anyone.

The judge may err, he may not succeed in discovering what is required by the rationale of the existing order, or he may be misled by his preference for a particular outcome of the case in hand; but all this does not alter the fact that he has a problem to solve for which in most instances there will be only one right solution and that this is a task in which his 'will' or his emotional response has no place. If often his 'intuition' rather than ratiocination will lead him to the right solution, this does not mean that the decisive factors in determining the result are emotional rather than rational, any more than in the case of the scientist who also is normally led intuitively to the right hypothesis which he can only afterwards try to test. Like most other intellectual tasks, that of the judge is not one of logical deduction from a limited number of premises, but one of testing hypotheses at which he has arrived by processes only in part conscious. But although he may not know what led him in the first instance to think that a particular decision was right, he must stand by his decision only if he can rationally defend it against all objections that can be raised against it.

If the judge is committed to maintaining and improving a going order of action, and must take his standards from that order, this does not mean, however, that his aim is to preserve any *status quo* in the relations between particular men. It is, on the contrary, an essential attribute of the order which he serves that it can be maintained only by constant changes in the particulars; and the judge is concerned only with the abstract relations which must be preserved while the particulars change. Such a system of abstract relationships is not a constant network connecting particular elements but a network with an ever-changing particular content. Although to the judge an existing position will often provide a presumption of right, his task is as much to assist change as to preserve existing positions. He is concerned with a dynamic order which will be maintained only by continuous changes in the positions of particular people.

But although the judge is not committed to upholding a particular *status quo*, he is committed to upholding the principles on which the existing order is based. His task is indeed one which has meaning only within a spontaneous and abstract order of actions such as the market produces. He must thus be conservative in the sense only that he cannot serve any order that is determined not by rules of individual conduct but by the particular ends of authority. A judge cannot be concerned with the needs of particular persons or groups, or with 'reasons of state' or 'the will of government', or with any particular purposes which an order of actions may be expected to serve. Within any organization in which the individual actions must be judged by their serviceability to the particular ends at which it aims, there is no room for the judge. In an order like that of socialism in which whatever rules may govern individual actions are not independent of particular results, such rules will not be 'justiciable' because they will require a balancing of the particular interests affected in the light of their importance. Socialism is indeed largely a revolt against the impartial justice which considers only the conformity of individual actions to end-independent rules and which is not concerned with the effects of their application in particular instances. Thus a socialist judge would really be a contradiction in terms; for his persuasion must prevent him from applying only those general principles which underlie a spontaneous order of actions, and lead him to take into account considerations which have nothing to do with the justice of individual conduct. He may, of course, be a socialist privately, and keep his socialism out of the considerations which determine his decisions. But he could not act as a judge on socialist principles. We shall later see that this has long been concealed by the belief that instead of acting on principles of just individual conduct he might be guided by what is called 'social justice', a phrase which describes precisely that aiming at particular results for particular persons or groups which is impossible within a spontaneous order.

The socialist attacks on the system of private property have created a widespread belief that the order the judges are required to uphold under that system is an order which serves particular interests. But the justification of the system of several property is not the interest of the property holders. It serves as much the interest of those who at the moment own no property as that of those who do, since the development of the whole order of actions on which modern civilization depends was made possible only by the institution of property.

The difficulty many people feel about conceiving of the judge as serving an existing but always imperfect abstract order which is not intended to serve particular interests is resolved when we remember that it is only these abstract features of the order which can serve as the basis of the decisions of individuals in unforeseeable future conditions, and which therefore alone can determine an enduring order; and that they alone for this reason can constitute a true *common* interest of the members of a Great Society, who do not pursue any particular common purposes but merely desire appropriate means for the pursuit of their respective individual purposes. What the judge can be concerned with in creating law is therefore only improvement of those abstract and lasting features of an order of action which is given to him and which maintains itself through changes in the relation between the particulars, while certain relations between these relations (or relations of a still higher order) are preserved. 'Abstract' and 'lasting' mean in this context more or less the same, as in the long term view which the judge must take he can consider only the effect of the rules he lays down in an unknown number of future instances which may occur at some future time.

Conclusions

We may sum up the results of this chapter with the following description of the properties which will of necessity belong to the law as it emerges from the judicial process: it will consist of rules regulating the conduct of persons towards others, applicable to an unknown number of future instances and containing prohibitions delimiting the boundary of the protected domain of each person (or organized group of persons). Every rule of this kind will in intention be perpetual, though subject to revision in the light of better insight into its interaction with other rules; and it will be valid only as part of a system of mutually modifying rules. These rules will achieve their intended effect of securing the formation of an abstract order of actions only through their universal application, while their application in the particular instance cannot be said to have a specific purpose distinct from the purpose of the system of rules as a whole.

The manner in which this system of rules of just conduct is developed by the systematic application of a negative test of justice and the elimination or modification of such rules as do not satisfy this test we will have to consider further in Volume 2, chapter 8. Our next task, however, will be to consider what such rules of just conduct *cannot* achieve and in what respect the rules required for the purposes or organization differ from them. We shall see that those rules of the latter kind which must be deliberately laid down by a legislature for the organization of government and which constitute the chief occupation of the existing legislatures, can in their nature not be restricted by those considerations which guide and restrict the law-making power of the judge.

In the last resort the difference between the rules of just conduct which emerge from the judicial process, the *nomos* or law of liberty considered in this chapter, and the rules of organization laid down by authority which we shall have to consider in the next chapter, lies in the fact that the former are derived from the conditions of a spontaneous order which man has not made, while the latter serve the deliberate building of an organization serving specific purposes. The former are *discovered* either in the sense that they merely articulate already observed practices or in the sense that they are found to be required complements of the already established rules if the order which rests on them is to operate smoothly and efficiently. They would never have been discovered if the existence of a spontaneous order of actions had not set the judges their peculiar task, and they are therefore rightly considered as something existing independently of a particular human will; while the rules of organization aiming at particular results will be free inventions of the designing mind of the organizer.

SIX

THESIS: THE LAW OF LEGISLATION

> The judge addresses himself to standards of consistency,
> equivalence, predictability, the legislator to fair shares, social
> utility and equitable distribution.
>
> Paul A. Freund*

Legislation originates from the necessity of establishing rules of organization

While in political theory the making of law has traditionally been represented as the chief function of legislative bodies, their origin and main concern had little to do with *the law* in the narrow sense in which we have considered it in the last chapter. This is especially true of the Mother of Parliaments: the English legislature arose in a country where longer than elsewhere the rules of just conduct, the common law, were supposed to exist independently of political authority. As late as the seventeenth century, it could still be questioned whether parliament could make law inconsistent with the common law. [1] The chief concern of what we call legislatures has always been the control and regulation of government, [2] that is the direction of an organization—and of an organization only one of whose aims was to see that the rules of just conduct were obeyed.

As we have seen, rules of just conduct did not need to be deliberately made, though men gradually learned to improve or change them deliberately. Government, by contrast, is a deliberate contrivance which, however, beyond its simplest and most primitive forms, also cannot be conducted exclusively by *ad hoc* commands of the ruler. As the organization which a ruler builds up to preserve peace and to keep out external enemies, and gradually to provide an increasing number of other services, becomes more and more distinct from the more comprehensive society comprising all the private activities of the citizens, it will require distinct rules of its own which determine its structure, aims, and functions. Yet these rules governing the apparatus of government will necessarily possess a character different from that of the universal rules of just conduct which form the basis of the spontaneous order of society at large. They will be rules of organization designed to achieve particular ends, to supplement positive orders that something should be done or that particular results should be achieved, and to set up for these purposes the various agencies through which government operates. They will be subsidiary to particular commands that indicate the ends to be pursued and the tasks of the different agencies. Their application to a particular case will depend on the particular task assigned to the particular agency and on the momentary ends of government. And they will have to establish a hierarchy of command determining the responsibilities and the range of discretion of the different agents.

This would be true even of an organization which had no task other than the enforcement of the rules of just conduct. Even in such an organization in which the rules of just conduct to be enforced by it were regarded as given, a different set of rules would have to govern its operation. The laws of procedure and the laws setting up the organization of the courts consist in this sense of rules of organization and not of rules of just conduct. Though these rules also aim at securing justice, and in early stages of development at a justice to be 'found', and therefore perhaps in earlier stages of development were more important for the achievement of justice than the rules of just conduct already explicitly formulated, they are yet logically distinct from the latter.

But if, with regard to the organization set up to enforce justice, the distinction between the rules defining just conduct and the rules regulating the enforcement of such conduct is often difficult to draw—and if indeed, the rules of just conduct may be defined only as those which would be found through a certain procedure—with regard to the other services which were gradually assumed by the apparatus of government it is clear that these will be governed by rules of another kind, rules which regulate the powers of the agents of government over the material and personal resources entrusted to them, but which need not give them power over the private citizen.

Even an absolute ruler could not do without laying down some general rules to take care of details. The extent of the powers of a ruler were, however, normally not unlimited but depended on a prevailing opinion of what were his rights. Since the law which it was his duty to enforce was regarded as given once and for all, it was chiefly with regard to the extent and exercise of his other powers that he often found it necessary to seek the consent and support of bodies representing the citizens.

Thus even when the *nomos* was regarded as given and more or less unchangeable, the ruler would often need authorization for special *measures* for which he wanted the collaboration of his subjects. The most important of such measures would be taxation, and it was from the need to obtain consent to taxes that parliamentary institutions arose.[3] The representative bodies called in for this purpose were thus from the beginning concerned primarily with governmental matters rather than with giving law in the narrow sense; though they might also be asked to testify as to what the recognized rules of just conduct were. But since the enforcement of the law was regarded as the primary task of government, it was natural that all the rules which governed its activities came to be called by the same name. This tendency was probably assisted by a desire of governments to confer on its rules of organization the same dignity and respect which *the law* commanded.

Law and statute: the enforcement of law and the execution of commands

There is no single term in English which clearly and unambiguously distinguishes any prescription which has been made, or 'set' or 'posited' by authority from one which is generally accepted without awareness of its source. Sometimes we can speak of an 'enactment', while the more familiar term 'statute' is usually confined to enactments which contain more or less general rules.[4] When we need a precise single term we shall occasionally employ the Greek word *thesis* to describe such 'set' law.

Because the chief activity of all legislatures has always been the direction of government, it was generally true that 'for lawyer's law Parliament has neither time nor taste'.[5] It would not have mattered if this had led only to lawyer's law being neglected by the legislatures and its development left to the courts. But it often led to the lawyer's law being changed incidentally and even inadvertently in the course of decisions on governmental measures and therefore in the service of particular purposes. Any decision of the legislature which touches on matters regulated by the *nomos* will, at least for the case in hand, alter and supersede that law. As a governing body the legislature is not bound by any law, and what it says concerning particular matters has the same force as a general rule and will supersede any such existing rule.

The great majority of the resolutions passed by representative assemblies do not of course lay down rules of just conduct but direct measures of government. This was probably so at all times. [6] Of British legislation it could be said in 1901: 'nine-tenths of each annual volume of statutes are concerned with what may be called administrative law; and an analysis of the content of the General Acts during the last four centuries would probably show a similar proportion.' [7]

The difference in meaning between 'law' as it is applied to the *nomos* and 'law' as it is used for all the other *theseis* which emerge from legislation, comes out most clearly if we consider how differently the 'law' relates to its application in the two cases. A rule of conduct cannot be 'carried out' or 'executed' as one carries out an instruction. One can obey the former or enforce obedience to it; but a rule of conduct merely limits the range of permitted action and usually does not determine a particular action; and what it prescribes is never accomplished but remains a standing obligation on all. Whenever we speak of 'carrying out a law' we mean by the term 'law' not a *nomos* but a *thesis* instructing somebody to do particular things. It follows that the 'law-giver' whose laws are to be 'executed' stands in a wholly different relation to those who are to execute them from the relation in which a 'law-giver' who prescribes rules of just conduct stands to those who have to observe them. The first kind of rules will be binding only on the members of the organization which we call government, while the latter will restrict the range of permitted actions for any member of the society. The judge who applies the law and directs its enforcement does not 'execute' it in the sense in which an administrator carries out a measure, or in which the 'executive' has to carry out the decision of the judge.

A statute (*thesis*) passed by a legislature *may* have all the attributes of a *nomos*, and is likely to have them if deliberately modelled after the *nomos*. But it *need* not, and in most of the cases where legislation is wanted it cannot have this character. In this chapter we shall consider further only those contents of enactments or *theses* which are not rules of just conduct. There is, as the legal positivists have always emphasized, indeed no limit to what can be put into a statute. But though such 'law' has to be executed by those to whom it is addressed, it does not thereby become law in the sense of rules of just conduct.

Legislation and the theory of the separation of powers

The confusion resulting from this ambiguity of the word 'law' is to be seen already in the earliest discussion of the principle of the separation of powers. When in these discussions 'legislation' is referred to, it seems at first to mean exclusively the laying down of universal rules of just conduct. But such rules of just conduct are of course not 'carried out' by the executive but are applied by the courts to particular litigations as they come before them; what the executive will have to carry out will be the decisions of the court. Only with regard to law in the second sense, namely enactments that do not establish universal rules of conduct but give instructions to government, will the 'executive' have to carry out what the legislature has resolved. Here, then, 'execution' is not execution of a rule (which makes no sense) but the execution of an instruction emanating from the 'legislature'.

The term 'legislature' is historically closely associated with the theory of the separation of powers and indeed became current only at about the time when this theory was first conceived. The belief which one still often encounters that the theory arose from a misinterpretation by Montesquieu of the British constitution of his time is certainly not correct. Although it is true that the actual constitution of Britain then did not conform to that principle, there can be no question that it did then govern political opinion in England[8] and had gradually been gaining acceptance in the great debates of the preceding century. What is important for our purposes is that even in those seventeenth-century discussions it was clearly realized that to conceive of legislation as a distinct activity presupposes an independent definition of what was meant by law, and that the term legislation would become vacuous if everything the legislature prescribed were to be called law. The idea that came to be more and more clearly expressed was that 'not only was law to be couched in general terms, but also the legislature must be restricted to the making of law, and not itself meddle with particular cases'.[9] In the *First Agreement of the People* of 1647 it was explicitly provided 'that in all laws made or to be made every person may be bound alike and that no tenure, estate, character, degree, birth, or place do confer any exemption from the ordinary course of procedure whereunto others are subjected'. [10] And in an 'official defence' of the *Instrument of Government* of 1653 the separation of powers is represented as 'the grand secret of liberty and good government'. [11] Although none of the seventeenth-century endeavours to embody this conception in a constitutional government succeeded, it gained increasing acceptance and John Locke's view clearly was that 'legislative authority is to act *in a particular way* . . . [and] those who wield this authority should make only general rules. They are to govern by promulgated established laws, not to be varied in particular cases.' [12] This became accepted British opinion in the eighteenth century and from it Montesquieu derived his account of the British constitution. The belief was shaken only when in the nineteenth century the conceptions of the Philosophical Radicals and particularly Bentham's demand for an omnicompetent legislature [13] led James Mill to substitute for the ideal of a government under the law the ideal of a government controlled by a popular assembly, free to take any particular action which that assembly approved. [14]

The governmental functions of representative assemblies

If we are not to be misled by the word 'legislature', therefore, we shall have to remember that it is no more than a sort of courtesy title conferred on assemblies which had primarily arisen as instruments of representative *government*. Modern legislatures clearly derive from bodies which existed before the deliberate making of rules of just conduct was even considered possible, and the latter task was only later entrusted to institutions habitually concerned with very different tasks. The noun 'legislature' does not in fact appear before the middle of the seventeenth century and it seems doubtful whether it was then applied to the existing 'constituted bodies' (to use R. A. Palmer's useful term [15]) as a result of a dimly perceived conception of a separation of powers, or, rather, in a futile attempt to restrict bodies claiming control over government to the making of general laws. However that may be, they were in fact never so confined, and 'legislature' has become simply a name for representative assemblies occupied chiefly with directing or controlling government.

The few attempts that were made to restrict those 'legislatures' to law-making in the narrow sense were bound to fail since they constituted an attempt to limit the only existing representative bodies to the laying down of general rules, and to deprive them of control over most of the activities of government. A good illustration of such an attempt is provided by a statement ascribed to Napoleon I, who is reported to have argued that: [16]

> Nobody can have greater respect for the independence of the legislative power than I: but legislation does not mean finance, criticism of the administration, or ninety-nine of the hundred things which in England the Parliament occupies itself with. The legislature should *legislate*, i.e., construct good laws on scientific principles of jurisprudence, but it must respect the independence of the executive as it desires its own independence to be respected.

This is of course the view of the function of legislatures which corresponds to Montesquieu's conception of the separation of powers; and it would have suited Napoleon's book because it would have confined the powers of the only existing representatives of the people to laying down general rules of just conduct and have deprived them of all powers over government. For the same reason it has appealed to others such as G. W. F. Hegel [17] and, more recently, W. Hasbach. [18] But the same reason made it unacceptable to all advocates of popular or democratic government. At the same time, however, the use of the name 'legislature' seems to have appeared attractive to them for another reason: it enabled them to claim for a predominantly governmental body that unlimited or 'sovereign' power which, according to traditional opinion, belonged only to the maker of law in the narrow sense of the term. Thus it came about that governmental assemblies, whose chief activities were of the kind which ought to be limited by law, became able to command whatever they pleased simply by calling their commands 'laws'.

It must be recognized, however, that, if popular or representative government was wanted, the only representative bodies which existed could not have submitted to the limitation which the ideal of separation of powers imposed upon legislatures proper. Such limitation need not have meant that the representative body exercising governmental powers must be exempt from law other than of its own making. It might have meant that in performing its purely governmental function it was confined by general laws laid down by another body, equally representative or democratic, which derived its supreme authority from its commitment to universal rules of conduct. On the lower echelons of government we have in fact numerous kinds of regional or local representative bodies which in their actions are thus subject to general rules which they cannot alter; and there is no reason why this should not apply also to the highest of all representative bodies directing government. Indeed, only thus could the ideal of government under the law be realized.

It will be useful at this point briefly to interrupt our main argument to consider a certain ambiguity of the concept of 'government'. Although the term covers a wide range of activities which in any orderly society are necessary or desirable, it also carries certain overtones that are inimical to the ideal of freedom under the law. There are, as we have seen, two distinct tasks included under it which must be distinguished: the enforcement of the universal rules of just conduct on the one hand, and, on the other, the direction of the organization built up to provide various services for the citizens at large.

It is in connection with the second group of activities that the term 'government' (and still more the verb 'governing') carries misleading connotations. The unquestioned need for a government that enforces the law and directs an organization providing many other services does not mean, in ordinary times, that the private citizen need be governed in the sense in which the government directs the personal and material resources entrusted to it for rendering services. It is usual today to speak of a government 'running a country' as if the whole society were an organization managed by it. Yet what really depends on it are chiefly certain conditions for the smooth running of those services that the countless individuals and organizations render to each other. These spontaneously ordered activities of the members of society certainly could and would go on even if all the activities peculiar to government temporarily ceased. Of course, in modern times government has in many countries taken over the direction of so many essential services, especially in the field of transport and communication, that the economic life would soon be paralysed if all government-directed services ceased. But this is so not because these services *can* be provided only by government, but because government has assumed the exclusive right to provide them.

Private law and public law

The distinction between universal rules of just conduct and the rules of organization of government is closely related to, and sometimes explicitly equated with, the distinction between private and public law. [19] What we have said so far, then, might be summed up by the statement that the law of legislation consists predominantly of public law. There does not exist, however, general agreement on exactly where the line of distinction between private and public law is to be drawn. The tendency of modern developments has been increasingly to blur this distinction by, on the one hand, exempting governmental agencies from the general rules of just conduct and, on the other, subjecting the conduct of private individuals and organizations to special purpose-directed rules, or even to special commands or permissions by administrative agencies. During the last hundred years it has been chiefly in the service of so-called 'social' aims that the distinction between rules of just conduct and rules for the organization of the services of government has been progressively obliterated.

For our purpose we shall henceforth regard the distinction between private and public law as being equivalent to the distinction between rules of just conduct and rules of organization (and in doing so, in conformity with predominant Anglo-Saxon but contrary to continental-European practice, place criminal law under private rather than public law). It must, however, be pointed out that the familiar terms 'private' and 'public' law can be misleading. Their similarity to the terms private and public welfare is apt to suggest wrongly that private law serves only the welfare of particular individuals and only the public law the general welfare. Even the classical Roman definition, according to which private law aims at the utility of individuals and public law at the condition of the Roman nation, [20] lends itself to such an interpretation. The suggestion that only public law aims at the public welfare is, however, correct only if 'public' is interpreted in a special narrow sense, namely as what concerns the organization of government, and if the term 'public welfare' is therefore not understood to be synonymous with general welfare, but is applied only to those particular aims with which the organization of government is directly concerned.

To regard only the public law as serving general welfare and the private law as protecting only the selfish interests of the individuals would be a complete inversion of the truth: it is an error to believe that only actions which deliberately aim at common purposes serve common needs. The fact is rather that what the spontaneous order of society provides for us is more important for everyone, and therefore for the general welfare, than most of the particular services which the organization of government can provide, excepting only the security provided by the enforcement of the rules of just conduct. A very prosperous and peaceful society is conceivable in which government confines itself to the last task; and for a long time, especially during the Middle Ages, the phrase *utilitas publica* indeed meant no more than that peace and justice which the enforcement of rules of just conduct secures. What is true is merely that the public law as the law of the organization of government requires those to whom it applies to serve deliberately the public interest, while the private law allows the individuals to pursue their respective individual ends and merely aims at so confining individual action that they will in the result serve the general interest.

The law of organization of government is not law in the sense of rules defining what kind of conduct is generally right, but consists of directions concerning what particular officers or agencies of government are required to do. They would more appropriately be described as the regulations or by-laws of government. Their aim is to authorize particular agencies to take particular actions for specified purposes, for which they are assigned particular means. But in a free society, these means do not include the private citizen. If these regulations of the organization of government are widely regarded as being rules of the same sort as the rules of just conduct, this is due to the circumstance that they emanate from the same authority which possesses also the power to prescribe rules of just conduct. They are called 'laws' as a result of an attempt to claim for them the same dignity and respect which is attached to the universal rules of just conduct. Thus governmental agencies were able to claim the obedience of the private citizen to particular commands aimed at the achievement of specific purposes.

The task of organizing particular services necessarily produces an entirely different conception of the nature of the rules to be laid down from that produced by the task of providing rules as the foundation of a spontaneous order. Yet it is the attitude fostered by the former which has come to dominate the conception of the aims of legislation. Since the deliberate construction of rules is concerned mainly with rules or organization, the thinking about the general principles of legislation has also fallen almost entirely into the hands of public lawyers, that is of the specialists in organization who often have so little sympathy with lawyer's law that one hesitates to describe them as lawyers. It is they who in modern times have almost wholly dominated the philosophy of law and who, through providing the conceptual framwork of all legal thinking and through their influence on judicial decisions, have profoundly affected also the private law. The fact that jurisprudence (especially on the European continent) has been almost entirely in the hands of public lawyers, who think of law primarily as public law, and of order entirely as organization, is chiefly responsible for the sway not only of legal positivism (which in the field of private law just does not make sense) but also of the socialist and totalitarian ideologies implicit in it.

Constitutional law

To the rules which we are in the habit of calling 'law' but which are rules of organization and not rules of just conduct belong in the first instance all those rules of the allocation and limitation of the powers of government comprised in the law of the constitution. They are commonly regarded as the 'highest' kind of law to which a special dignity attaches, or to which more reverence is due than to other law. But, although there are historical reasons which explain this, it would be more appropriate to regard them as a super-structure erected to secure the maintenance of *the law*, rather than, as they are usually represented, as the source of all other law.

The reason why a particular dignity and fundamental character is attributed to the laws of the constitution is that, just because they had to be formally agreed upon, a special effort was required to confer on them the authority and respect which *the law* had long enjoyed. Usually the outcome of a long struggle, they were known to have been achieved at a high price in the comparatively recent past. They were seen as the result of conscious agreement that ended long strife and was often ceremoniously sworn to, consisting of principles whose infringement would revive sectional conflict or even civil war. Frequently they were also documents which for the first time conceded equal rights as full citizens to a numerous and hitherto oppressed class.

Nothing of this, however, alters the fact that a constitution is essentially a superstructure erected over a pre-existing system of law to organize the enforcement of that law. Although, once established, it may seem 'primary'[21] in the logical sense that now the other rules derive their authority from it, it is still intended to support these pre-existing rules. It creates an instrument to secure law and order and to provide the apparatus for the provision of other services, but it does not define what law and justice are. It is also true, as has been well said, that 'public law passes but private law persists'. [22] Even when as a result of revolution or conquest the whole structure of government changes, most of the rules of just conduct, the civil and criminal law, will remain in force—even in cases where the desire to change some of them may have been the main cause of the revolution. This is so because only by satisfying general expectations can a new government obtain the allegiance of its subjects and thereby become 'legitimate'.

Even when a constitution, in determining the power of the different organs of government, limits the power of the law-making assembly proper, as I believe every constitution should and early constitutions intended to do, and when for this purpose it defines the formal properties which a law must possess in order to be valid, such a definition of rules of just conduct would itself not be a rule of just conduct. It would provide what H. L. A. Hart has called a 'rule of recognition', [23] enabling the courts to ascertain whether particular rules possess those properties or not; but it would not itself be a rule of just conduct. Nor would such definition by the rules of recognition alone confer on the pre-existing law its validity. It would provide a guide for the judge, but, like all attempts to articulate conceptions underlying an existing system of norms, it might prove inadequate, and the judge might still have to go beyond (or restrict) the literal meaning of the words employed.

In no other part of public law is there greater resistance to the denying to it the attributes of rules of just conduct than in constitutional law. It seems that to most students of the subject the contention that the law of the constitution is not law in the sense in which we describe the rules of just conduct as law has appeared to be just outrageous and not to be deserving of consideration. Indeed for this reason the most prolonged and searching attempts to arrive at a clear distinction between the two kinds of law, those made in Germany during the later part of the last century concerning what was then called law in the 'material' (or 'substantive') and law in the merely 'formal' sense, could not lead to any result; for none of the participating writers could bring themselves to accept what they saw as the inevitable but, as they thought, absurd conclusion, namely that constitutional law would, on any sensible principle of distinction, have to be classed with the law in the merely formal and not with law in the material sense. [24]

Financial legislation

The field in which the difference between rules of just conduct and other products of legislation stands out most clearly, and where in consequence it was recognized early that the 'political laws' concerning it were something different from the 'juridical laws', was the field in which 'legislation' by representative bodies had first appeared—that is, finance. There is in this field indeed a difficult and important distinction to be made between the authorization of expenditure and the determination of the manner in which the burden is to be apportioned between the different individuals and groups. But that, taken as a whole, a government budget is a plan of action for an organization, conferring authority on particular agencies to do particular things, and not a statement of rules of just conduct, is fairly obvious. In fact, most of a budget, so far as it concerns expenditure, will not contain any rules at all, [25] but will consist of instructions concerning the purposes and the manner in which the means at the disposal of government are to be used. Even the German scholars of the last century who tried so hard to claim for public law the character of what they called 'law in the material sense' had to stop here and to admit that the budget could in no way be brought under that heading. A representative assembly approving such a plan of operation of government clearly acts not as a legislature in the sense in which this term is understood, for example in the conception of the separation of powers, but as the highest organ of government, giving instructions which the executive has to carry out.

This is not to say that in all those actions governed by 'legislative' instructions government ought not also, in the same manner as any other person or agency, to be subject to general rules of just conduct, and in particular be required to respect the private domains defined by those rules. Indeed, the belief that these instructions to government, because they are also called laws, supersede or modify the general rules applicable to everybody, is the chief danger against which we ought to guard ourselves by clearly distinguishing between the two kinds of 'laws'. This becomes evident if we turn from the expenditure side to the revenue side of the budget. The determination of the total revenue to be raised by taxation in a particular year is still a particular decision to be guided by particular circumstances—though whether a burden that a majority is willing to bear may also be imposed on a minority unwilling to do so, or how a given total burden is to be apportioned between the different persons and groups, does raise questions of justice. Here too, then, the obligations of the individuals ought to be governed by general rules, applicable irrespective of the particular size of the expenditure decided upon—indeed by rules which ought to be unalterably given to those who have to decide on expenditure. We are so used to a system under which expenditure is decided upon first and the question of who is to bear the burden considered afterwards, that it is rarely recognized how much this conflicts with the basic principle of limiting all coercion to the enforcement of rules of just conduct.

Administrative law and the police power

Much the greatest part of what is called public law, however, consists of administrative law, that is the rules regulating the activities of the various governmental agencies. So far as these rules determine the manner in which these agencies are to use the personal and material resources placed at their disposal, they are obviously rules of organization similar to those which any large organization will need. They are of special interest only because of the public accountability of those to whom they are applied. The term 'administrative law' is, however, used also with two other meanings.

It is used to describe the regulations laid down by administrative agencies and which are binding not only for the officers of these agencies but also for private citizens dealing with these agencies. Such regulations will clearly be required to determine the use of the various services or facilities provided by government for the citizens, but they often extend beyond this and supplement the general rules delimiting private domains. In the latter case they constitute delegated legislation. There may be good reasons for leaving the determination of some such rules to regional or local bodies. The question whether such rule-making powers should be delegated only to representative bodies or may also be entrusted to bureaucratic agencies, although important, does not concern us here. All that is relevant in the present context is that in this capacity 'administrative legislation' ought to be subject to the same limitations as the true law-making power of the general legislature.

The term 'administrative law' is further used to describe 'administrative powers over persons and property', not consisting of universal rules of just conduct but aiming at particular foreseeable results, and therefore necessarily involving discrimination and discretion. It is in connection with administrative law in this sense that a conflict with the concept of freedom under the law arises. In the legal tradition of the English-speaking world it used to be assumed that in their relation to the private citizens the administrative authorities were under the same rules of general (common or statute) law and subject to the same jurisdiction of the ordinary courts as any private citizen. It was only with respect to administrative law in the sense last mentioned, that is, different law applying to the relations between government agencies and citizens, that A. V. Dicey could maintain, as late as the beginning of this century, that it did not exist in Great Britain [26]—twenty years after foreign authors had written long treatises on British administrative law in the sense discussed before. [27]

As the services which government renders to the citizens develop, a need for regulations of the use of these services obviously arises. The conduct on roads and other public places provided for general use cannot be regulated by the assignment of individual domains but requires rules determined by consideration of expediency. Though such rules for the use of institutions provided for the public will be subject to requirements of justice (mainly in the sense that they ought to be the same for all) they do not aim at justice. The government in laying down such rules will have to be just, but not the persons who are to obey the rules. The 'rule of the road', requiring that we drive on the left or on the right, etc., which is often quoted as an illustration of a general rule, is therefore not really an example of a true rule of just conduct. [28] Like other rules for the use of public institutions, it ought to be the same for all, or at least aim at securing the same benefits for all users, but it does not define just conduct.

Such regulations for the use of public places or institutions are rules aiming at particular results, although they ought not, if intended to serve the 'general welfare', to aim at benefiting particular groups. Yet they may well, as is obvious in the case of traffic regulations, require that agents of government be given power of specific direction. When the police are given authority to do what is necessary to maintain public order, this refers essentially to securing orderly conduct in public places where the individual cannot have as much freedom as is assured to him in his private domain; special measures may here be needed to secure, for example the unimpeded flow of traffic. Government, mostly local government, is given the task of maintaining facilities in working order in such a way that the public can use them most efficiently for its purposes.

There has been a tendency, however, to interpret 'public places' not merely as facilities provided by government for the public, but as any place where the public congregates, even if they are provided commercially, such as department stores, factories, theatres, sports grounds, etc. While there is undoubtedly need for general rules which assure the safety and health of users of such places, it is not obvious that for this purpose a discretionary 'police power' is required. It is significant that so long as the basic ideal of the rule of law was still respected 'British factory legislation', for instance, 'found it possible to rely practically altogether on general rules (although to a large extent framed by administrative regulations)'. [29]

The 'measures' of policy

Where government is concerned with providing particular services, most of them of the kind which have recently come to be described as the 'infrastructure' of the economic system, the fact that such services will often aim at particular effects raises difficult problems. Particular actions of this sort are usually described as 'measures' of policy (especially on the continent by the corresponding terms *mesures* or *Massnahmen*) and it will be convenient to consider some of those problems under this heading. The crucial point has been well expressed by the statement that there can be no 'equality before a measure' as there is equality before the law. [30] What is meant by this is that most measures of this sort will be 'aimed', in the sense that, although their effects cannot be confined to those who are prepared to pay for the services provided by them, they will yet benefit only some more or less clearly discernible group and not all citizens equally. Probably most of the services rendered by government, other than the enforcement of just conduct, are of this sort. The problems which arise can be solved only partially by leaving such services largely to local government or special regional governmental agencies created for a specific purpose, such as water-boards and the like.

The defraying out of a common purse of the costs of services which will benefit only some of those who have contributed to it will usually be agreed upon by the rest only on the understanding that other requirements of theirs will be met in the same manner, so that a rough correspondence of burdens to benefits will result. In the discussion of the organization of such services with approximately determinable beneficiaries, particular interests will regularly be in conflict and a reconciliation will only be attainable by a compromise—which is quite different from what happens in a discussion of general rules of conduct that aim at an abstract order with largely unpredictable benefits. Thus it is so important that the authorities who will be in charge of such matters, even if they are democratic or representative bodies, should, in determining particular services, be subject to general rules of conduct and not be in a position themselves 'to rewrite the rules of the game as they go along'.[31]

When we speak of administrative measures, we generally mean the direction of particular resources towards the rendering of certain services to determinable groups of people. The establishment of a system of schools or health services, financial or other assistance to particular trades or professions, or the use of such instruments as government possesses through its monopoly of the issue of money, are in this sense measures of policy. It is evident that in connection with such measures the distinction between providing facilities to be used by unknown persons for unknown purposes, and providing facilities in the expectation that they will help particular groups, becomes a matter of degree, with many intermediate positions between the two extreme types. No doubt if government became the exclusive provider of many essential services, it could, by determining the character of these services and the conditions on which they are rendered, exercise great influence on the material content of the order of the market. For this reason it is important that the size of this 'public sector' be limited and the government do *not* so co-ordinate its various services that their effects on particular people become predictable. We shall later see that it is also important for this reason that government have no *exclusive* right to the rendering of any service other than the enforcement of rules of just conduct, and thus should not be in a position to prevent other agencies from offering services of the same kind when possibilities appear of providing through the market what perhaps in the past has been impossible thus to provide.

*The transformation of private law into public law by 'social'
legislation*

If in the course of the last hundred years the principle that in a
free society coercion is permissible only to secure obedience to
universal rules of just conduct has been abandoned, this was done
mainly in the service of what were called 'social' aims. 'Social' as
used here, however, covers various kinds of concepts which must
be carefully distinguished.

In the first instance it meant chiefly the removal of discrimina-
tions by law which had crept in as a result of the greater influence
that certain groups like landlords, employers, creditors, etc., had
wielded on the formation of the law. This does not mean, however,
that the only alternative is instead to favour the class treated un-
fairly in the past, and that there is not a 'mean' position in which
the law treats both parties alike according to the same principles.
Equal treatment in this sense has nothing to do with the question
whether the application of such general rules in a particular situation may lead to *results* which are more favourable to one group than
to the others: justice is not concerned with the results of the various
transactions but only with whether the transactions themselves are
fair. Rules of just conduct cannot alter the fact that, with perfectly
just behaviour on both sides, the low productivity of labour in some
countries will bring about a situation where the wages at which all
can get employment will be very low—and at the same time the
return on capital will be very high—and where higher wages could
be secured to some only by means which would prevent others from
finding employment at all.

We shall see later that justice in this connection can mean only
such wages or prices as have been determined in a free market
without deception, fraud or violence; and that, in this one sense in
which we can talk meaningfully about just wages or just prices, the
result of a wholly just transaction may indeed be that one side gets
very little out of it and the other a great deal. Classical liberalism
rested on the belief that there existed discoverable principles of
just conduct of universal applicability which could be recognized as
just irrespective of the effects of their application on particular
groups.

'Social legislation', second, may refer to the provision by government of certain services which are of special importance to some
unfortunate minorities, the weak or those unable to provide for

themselves. Such service functions of government a wealthy community may decide to provide for a minority—either on moral grounds or as an insurance against contingencies which may affect anybody. Although the provision of such services increases the necessity of levying taxes, these can be raised according to uniform principles; and the duty to contribute to the costs of such agreed common aims could be brought under the conception of general rules of conduct. It would not make the private citizen in any way the object of administration; he would still be free to use his knowledge for his purposes and not have to serve the purposes of an organization.

There is, however, a third kind of 'social' legislation. The aim of it is to direct private activity towards particular ends and to the benefit of particular groups. It was as the result of such endeavours, inspired by the will-o'-the-wisp of 'social justice', that the gradual transformation of the purpose-independent rules of just conduct (or the rules of private law) into purpose-dependent rules of organization (or rules of public law) has taken place. This pursuit of 'social justice' made it necessary for governments to treat the citizen and his property as an object of administration with the aim of securing particular results for particular groups. When the aim of legislation is higher wages for particular groups of workers, or higher incomes for small farmers, or better housing for the urban poor, it cannot be achieved by improving the general rules of conduct.

Such endeavours towards a 'socialization' of the law have been taking place in most Western countries for several generations and have already gone far to destroy the characteristic attribute of universal rules of conduct, the equality of all under the same rules. The history of such legislation which began in Germany in the last century under the name *Sozialpolitik* and spread first to the continent and England, and in this century also to the United States, cannot be sketched here. Some of the landmarks in this development which led to the creation of special rules for particular classes are the English Trade Disputes Act of 1906 which conferred on the labour unions unique privileges, [32] and the decisions of the U.S. Supreme Court during the earlier period of the New Deal which conceded to legislatures unlimited powers to 'safeguard the vital interests of the people', [33] saying in effect that for any end a legislature regarded as beneficial it might pass any law it liked.

The country in which this development went further and its

consequences were most fully accepted and explicitly recognized remained, however, the country in which it started. In Germany it had come to be widely understood that the pursuit of these social aims involved the progressive replacement of private law by public law. Indeed, the leaders of socialist thought in the field of law openly pronounced the doctrine that the private law aiming at the co-ordination of individual activities would progressively be replaced by a public law of subordination, and that 'for a social order of law private law was to be regarded only as a provisional and constantly decreasing range of private initiative, temporarily spared within the all-comprehensive sphere of public law'. [34] In Germany this development was much facilitated by a surviving tradition of a fundamentally unlimited power of government, based on a mystique of *Hoheit* and *Herrschaft*, which found its expression in conceptions, then still largely unintelligible in the Western world, such as that the citizen is the subject of the administration, and that administrative law is 'the law peculiar to the relations between the administering state and the subjects it encounters in its activities'. [35]

The mental bias of a legislature preoccupied with government

All this raises questions which will be our main concern in the second volume of this work. Here we can touch on them only briefly to indicate the reasons why the confounding of the making of rules of just conduct with the direction of the government apparatus tends to produce a progressive transformation of the spontaneous order of society into an organization. Only a few preliminary remarks need be added on the altogether different mental attitude which the occupation with questions of organization will produce among the members of an assembly so occupied from that which would prevail in an assembly mainly occupied with law-giving in the classical sense of the term.

Increasingly and inevitably an assembly occupied in the former way tends to think of itself as a body that not merely provides some services for an independently functioning order but 'runs the country' as one runs a factory or any other organization. Since it possesses authority to arrange everything, it cannot refuse responsibility for anything. There will be no particular grievance which it will not be regarded as capable of removing; and since in every one particular instance taken by itself it will generally be capable of remedying such a grievance, it will be assumed that it can remove all grievances at the same time. However, it is a fact that most of the grievances of particular individuals or groups can be removed only by measures which create new grievances elsewhere.

An experienced British Labour parliamentarian has described the duty of the political as the removal of all sources of discontent. [36] This, of course, requires an arrangement of all particular matters in a manner no set of general rules of conduct can determine. But dissatisfaction does not necessarily mean legitimate dissatisfaction, nor does the existence of dissatisfaction prove that its source can be removed for all. Indeed, it is most likely to be due to circumstances which nobody could prevent or alter in accordance with generally accepted principles. The idea that the aim of government is the satisfaction of all particular wishes held by a sufficiently large number, without any limitation on the means which the representative body may use for this purpose, must lead to a condition of society in which all the particular actions are commanded in accordance with a detailed plan agreed upon through bargaining within a majority and then imposed on all as the 'common aim' to be realized.

NOTES

INTRODUCTION

* Guglielmo Ferrero, *The Principles of Power* (New York, 1942), p. 318. The paragraph from which the quotation is taken begins: 'Order is the exhausting Sisyphean labour of mankind against which mankind is always in a potential state of conflict . . .'

1 The time-honoured phrase widely used in the eighteenth and nineteenth centuries is 'limited constitution', but the expression 'limiting constitution' also occurs occasionally in the earlier literature.

2 See K. C. Wheare, *Modern Constitutions*, revised edition (Oxford, 1960), p. 202: 'the original idea behind [constitutions] is that of limiting government and of requiring those who govern to conform to laws and rules'; see also C. H. McIlwain, *Constitutionalism: Ancient and Modern*, revised edition (Ithaca, N.Y., 1958) p. 21: 'All constitutional government is by definition limited government . . . constitutionalism has one essential quality: it is a legal limitation of government; it is the antithesis of arbitrary rule; its opposite is despotic government, the government of will'; C. J. Friedrich, *Constitutional Government and Democracy* (Boston, 1941), especially p. 131, where a constitution is defined as 'the process by which governmental action is effectively restrained'.

3 See Richard Wollheim, 'A paradox in the theory of democracy', in Peter Laslett and W. G. Runciman (eds); *Philosophy, Politics and Society*, second series (Oxford, 1962), p. 72: 'the modern conception of Democracy is of a form of government in which no restriction is placed upon the governing body.'

4 See George Burdeau, 'Une Survivance: la notion de constitution', in *L'Evolution du droit public, études offertes à Achille Mestre* (Paris, 1956).

5 See F. A. Hayek, *The Constitution of Liberty* (London and Chicago, 1960).

6 See Samuel H. Beer, 'The British legislature and the problem of mobilizing consent,' in Elke Frank (ed), *Lawmakers in a Changing World* (Englewood Cliffs, N.J., 1966), and reprinted in B. Crick (ed), *Essays on Reform* (Oxford, 1967).

7 See F. A. Hayek, op. cit., p. 207 and note 12.

8 Torgny T. Segerstedt, 'Wandel der Gesellschaft', *Bild der Wissenschaft*, vol. vi, May 1969, p. 441.

9 Enrico Ferri, *Annales de l'Institut Internationale de Sociologie*, vol. i., 1895, p. 166: 'Le socialisme est le point d'arrivée logique et inévitable de la sociologie.'

CHAPTER ONE   REASON AND EVOLUTION

* Lord Acton, *The History of Freedom and Other Essays* (London, 1907), p. 58. Most of the problems to be discussed in this introductory chapter have been examined at somewhat greater length in a series of preliminary studies most of which have been reprinted in F. A. Hayek, *Studies in Philosophy, Politics and Economics* (London and Chicago, 1967) (henceforth referred to as *S.P.P.E.*): see, in particular, chapters 2–6 in that book as well as my lecture (1966) on Dr Bernard Mandeville, in *Proceedings of the British Academy*, lii (London, 1967), and *The Confusion of Language in Political Theory* (London, 1968).

1 It is the fashion today to sneer at any assertion that something is impossible and to point at the numerous instances in which what even scientists represented as impossible has later proved to be possible. Nevertheless, it is true that all advance of scientific knowledge consists in the last resort in the insight into the impossibility of certain events. Sir Edmund Whittaker, a mathematical physicist, has described this as the 'impotence principle' and Sir Karl Popper has systematically developed the idea that all scientific laws consist essentially of prohibitions, that is, of assertions that something cannot happen; see especially Karl Popper, *The Logic of Scientific Discovery* (London, 1954).

2 On the role played by Bernard Mandeville in this connection see my lecture on him quoted in the asterisked note at the beginning of this chapter.

3 The implications of at least the most widely held interpretation of the Cartesian approach for all moral and political problems are clearly brought out in Alfred Espinas, *Descartes et la morale*, 2 vols (Paris, 1925), especially at the beginning of vol 2. On the domination of the whole French Enlightenment by the Cartesian brand of rationalism, see G. de Rugiero, *History of European Liberalism*, trans. R. G. Collingwood (London, 1927), p. 21 *et seq.*:

> To the Cartesian school belong almost all the exponents of the higher and middle culture of the eighteenth century: the scientists, . . . the social reformers, drawing up their indictment against history as a museum of irrational uses and abuses, and endeavouring to reconstruct the whole social system; the jurists,

in whose eyes law is and must be a system deducible from a few universal and self-evident principles.

See also H. J. Laski, *Studies in Law and Politics* (London and New Haven, 1922), p. 20:

> What does rationalism [with regard to Voltaire, Montesquieu, etc.] mean? It is, essentially, an attempt to apply the principles of Cartesianism to human affairs. Take as postulates the inescapable evidence of stout common sense, and reason logically from them to the conclusions they imply. That common sense, all the philosophers believed, will give everywhere the same results: what it is to the sage of Ferney it will be in Peking or the woods of America.

4 Descartes himself gave expression to this attitude when he wrote in his *Discours de la méthode* (beginning of part 2) that 'the greatness of Sparta was due not to the pre-eminence of each of its laws in particular, . . . but to the circumstances that, originated by a single individual, they all tended to a single end.' For a characteristic application of this idea by an eighteenth-century ruler see the statement by Frederick II of Prussia quoted in G. Küntzel, *Die politischen Testamente der Hohenzollern* (Leipzig, 1920), vol 2, p. 64, where he maintains that, as little as Newton could have designed his system of universal attraction if he had had to collaborate with Leibniz and Descartes, could a political system originate and maintain itself if it were not the product of a single mind.

5 'Pragmatic' is the older expression used in this connection chiefly by Carl Menger, *Untersuchungen über die Methoden der Socialwissenschaften* (Leipzig, 1882), translated as *Problems of Economics and Sociology* by F. J. Nock, with an introduction by Louis Schneider (Urbana, Ill., 1963), which contains still the best earlier treatment of these problems.

6 On the decisive influence of Descartes on Rousseau see H. Michel, *L'Idée de l'état* (Paris, 1896), p. 66 (with references to earlier authors); A. Schatz, *L'Individualisme économique et social* (Paris, 1907), p. 40 *et seq.*; R. Derathé, *Le Rationalisme de Jean-Jacques Rousseau* (Paris, 1948); and the perceptive observation of R. A. Palmer, *The Age of Democratic Revolution* (Princeton, 1959 and 1964), vol 1, p. 114, that for Rousseau 'there was even no law except law willed by living men— this was his greatest heresy from many points of view, including the Christian: it was also his greatest affirmation in political theory.'

7 See R. S. Peters, *The Concept of Motivation* (London, 1959), p. 5:

> *Man is a rule-following animal.* His actions are not simply directed towards ends; they also conform to social standards and conventions, and unlike a calculating machine he acts because of his

knowledge of rules and objectives. For instance, we ascribe to people *traits* of character like honesty, punctuality, considerateness and meanness. Such terms do not, like ambition, or hunger, or social desire, indicate the sort of goals that a man tends to pursue; rather they indicate the type of regulations that he imposes on his conduct whatever his goals may be.

8 See F. A. Hayek, *The Constitution of Liberty* (London and Chicago, 1960), especially ch. 2.

9 J. A. Schumpeter, *History of Economic Analysis* (New York, 1954), p. 241.

10 See my lectures on 'Economics and knowledge' (1936) and 'The use of knowledge in society' (1945), both reprinted in F. A. Hayek, *Individualism and Economic Order* (London and Chicago, 1948).

11 The expression 'the Great Society', which we shall frequently use in the same sense in which we shall use Sir Karl Popper's term 'the Open Society', was, of course, already familiar in the eighteenth century (see for example Richard Cumberland, *A Treatise on the Law of Nature* (London, 1727), ch. 8 section 9, as well as Adam Smith and Rousseau) and in modern times was revived by Graham Wallas when he used it as the title for one of his books (*The Great Society* (London and New York, 1920)). It has probably not lost its suitability by its use as a political slogan by a recent American administration.

12 Lewis Mumford in his introduction to F. Mackenzie (ed), *Planned Society* (New York, 1937), p. vii: 'We have still to develop what Patrick Geddes used sometimes to call the art of simultaneous thinking: the ability to deal with a multitude of related phenomena at the same time, and of composing, in a single picture, both the qualitative and the quantitative attributes of these phenomena.'

13 Jane Jacobs, *The Death and Life of Great American Cities* (New York, 1961).

14 Perhaps the current uncritical enthusiasm about computers makes it advisable to mention that, however great their power of digesting facts fed into them, they do not help us in ascertaining these facts.

15 See A. M. Carr-Saunders, *The Population Problem: A Study in Human Evolution* (Oxford, 1922), p. 223:

> Men and groups of men are naturally selected on account of the customs they practise just as they are selected on account of their mental and physical characters. Those groups practising the most advantageous customs will have an advantage in the constant struggle between adjacent groups over those that practise less advantageous customs. Few customs can be more advantageous than those which limit the numbers of a group to the desirable number, and there is no difficulty in understanding how—once any of these three customs [abortion, infanticide, abstention from

intercourse] had originated it would, by a process of natural selection, come to be so practised that it would produce an approximation to the desirable number.

A very remarkable exposition of the basic idea is to be found in two essays by W. K. Clifford: 'On the scientific basis of morals' (1873) and 'Right and wrong: the scientific ground of their distinction' (1875), both reprinted in W. K. Clifford, *Lectures and Essays* (London, 1879), vol. 2, especially pp. 112–21 and 169–72, of which only some of the most relevant passages can be quoted here:

> Adaptation of means to an end may be produced in two ways that we at present know of: by process of natural selection, and by the agency of an intelligence in which an image or idea of the end preceded the use of the means. In both cases the existence of adaptation is accounted for by the necessity or utility of the end. It seems to me convenient to use the word *purpose* as meaning generally the end to which certain means are adapted, both in these two cases, and in any others that may hereafter become known, provided only that the adaptation is accounted for by the necessity of the end. And there seems to be no objection to the use of the phrase 'final cause' in this wider sense if it is to be kept at all. The word 'design' might then be kept for the special case of adaptation by intelligence. And we may then say that since the process of natural selection has been understood, *purpose* has ceased to suggest *design* to instructed people except in cases where the agency of men is independently probably [p. 117]. Those tribes have on the whole survived in which conscience approved of such actions as tended to the improvement of men's character as citizens and therefore to the survival of the tribe. Hence it is that the moral conscience of the individual, though founded upon the experience of the tribe, is purely intuitive: conscience gives no reasons [p. 119]. *Our sense of right and wrong is derived from such order as we can observe* [p. 121: my italics].

16 See A. M. Carr-Saunders, op. cit., p. 302: 'Mental characters are adapted to the whole of the traditional [as distinguished from the physical] environment. Men come to be selected in accordance with the needs of social organization, and as traditions grow in amount also in accordance with the capability of absorbing tradition.'; See also Peter Farb, *Man's Rise to Civilization* (New York, 1968), p. 13:

> In arriving at their varying ways of life, societies do not make conscious choices. Rather they make unconscious adaptations. Not all societies are presented with the same set of environmental conditions, nor are all societies at the same stage when these choices are presented. For various reasons, some societies adapt

to conditions in a certain way, some in a different way, and others not at all. Adaptation is not a conscious choice, and the people who make up a society do not quite understand what they are doing; they know only that a particular choice works, even though it may appear bizarre to outsiders.

See further, Alexander Alland, Jr, *Evolution and Human Behavior* (New York, 1967).

17 The decisive observation, in modern times first emphasized by Otto Jespersen in *Language, Its Nature, Development and Origin* (London, 1922), p. 130, was already mentioned by Adam Ferguson in *Principles of Moral and Political Science* (Edinburgh, 1792), vol. i, p. 7: 'The beautiful analogy of expression, on which the rules of grammar are established, is agreeable to the genius of man. Children are frequently misled by it, by following analogy where the practice actually deviates from it. Thus, a little boy, asked how he came by his plaything, said *Father buyed it for him.*'

18 See F. Heinimann, *Nomos and Physis* (Basel, 1945); John Burnet, 'Law and nature in Greek ethics', *International Journal of Ethics*, vii, 1893, and *Early Greek Philosophy*, fourth edition (London, 1930), p. 9; and particularly Karl R. Popper, *The Open Society and Its Enemies* (London and Princeton, 1945 and later), especially ch. 5.

19 Adam Ferguson, *An Essay on the History of Civil Society* (London, 1767), p. 187: 'Nations stumble upon establishments, which are indeed the result of human action, but not the execution of any human design.' In the introduction to his recent edition of this work (Edinburgh, 1966), p. xxiv, Duncan Forbes points out that:

Ferguson, like Smith, Millar, and others (but not Hume [?]), has dispensed with the 'Legislators and Founders of states', a superstition that Durkheim thought has hindered the development of social science more than anything else, and which is to be found even in Montesquieu. . . . The Legislator myth flourished in the eighteenth century, for a variety of reasons, and its destruction was perhaps the most original and daring *coup* of the social science of the Scottish Enlightenment.

20 See Sten Gagnèr, *Studien zur Ideengeschichte der Gesetzgebung* (Uppsala, 1960), pp. 208 and 242. It would thus seem that the whole confusion involved in the dispute between legal positivism and the theories of the law of nature trace back directly to the false dichotomy here discussed.

21 See ibid., p. 231, on Guillaume de Conches and particularly his statement: 'Et est positiva que est ab hominibus inventa ut suspensio latronis. Naturalis vero que non est homine inventa.'

22 Luis Molina, *De iustitia et iure* (Cologne, 1596–1600), tom. ll, disp.

347, no. 3: 'naturale dicitur, quoniam et ipsis rebus, seclusa quacumque humana lege et decreto consurgit, dependetur tamen ab multiis circumstantiis, quibus variatur, atque ab hominum affectu, ac aestimatione, comparatione diversum usum, interdum pro solo hominum beneplacito et arbitrio.' On Molina see Wilhelm Weber, *Wirtschaftsethik am Vorabend des Liberalismus* (Münster, 1959); and W. S. Joyce, 'The economics of Louis Molina' (1948), unpublished Ph.D. thesis, Harvard University.

23 Edmund Burke, *Reflections on the Revolution in France*, in *Works* (London, 1808) vol. 5, p. 437.

24 Johannes de Lugo, *Disputationum de iustitia et iure tomus secundus* (Lyon, 1642), disp. 26, section 4, No. 40: 'incertitudo ergo nostra circa pretium iustum Mathematicum . . . provenit ex Deo, quod non sciamus determinare'; see also Joseph Höffner, *Wirtschaftsethik und Monopole im fünfzehnten und sechzehnten Jahrhundert* (Jena, 1941), pp. 114–15.

25 As John Locke understood. See his *Essays on the Law of Nature* (1676), ed W. von Leyden (Oxford, 1954),

> By reason . . . I do not think is meant here that faculty of the understanding which forms trains of thought and deduces proofs, but certain definite principles of action from which spring all virtues and whatever is necessary for the proper moulding of morals . . . reason does not so much establish and pronounce this law of nature as search for it and discover it. . . . Neither is reason so much the maker of that law as its interpreter.

26 See Joseph Kohler, 'Die spanische Naturrechtslehre des 16. und 17. Jahrhunderts,' *Archiv für Rechts- und Wirtschaftsphilosophie*, x, 1916–17, especially p. 235; and in particular A. P. D'Entreves, *Natural Law* (London, 1951), pp. 51 *et seq.*, and the observation on p. 56 about 'how all of a sudden we are faced with a doctrine which purposely sets out to construe civil society as the result of a deliberate act of will on the part of its components.' See also John C. H. Wu, 'Natural law and our common law'. *Fordham Law Review*, xxiii, 1954, 21–2: 'The modern speculative, rationalistic philosophies of Natural Law are aberrations from the high road of scholastic tradition . . . . They proceed *more geometrico*'.

27 On Matthew Hale see in particular J. G. A. Pocock, *The Ancient Constitution and the Feudal Law* (Cambridge, 1957), Ch. 7.

28 See the significant observation by J. M. Guyau, *La Morale anglaise contemporaine* (Paris, 1879), p. 5:

> Les disciples de Bentham comparent leur maître à Descartes. 'Donnez-moi le matière et le mouvement', disait Descartes, 'et je ferai le monde'; mais Descartes ne parlait que du monde physique,

oeuvre inerte et insensible. . . . 'Donnez-moi', peut dire à
son tour Bentham, 'donnez-moi les affections humaines, la joie
et la douleur, la peine et le plaisir, et je créerai un monde moral.
Je produirai non seulement la justice, mais encore la generosité,
le patriotisme, la philanthropie, et toutes le vertues aimables
où sublimes dans leur pureté et leur exaltation.'

29 On the indirect influence of Edmund Burke on the German historical
school through the Hannoverian scholars Ernst Brandes and A. W.
Rehberg see H. Ahrens, *Die Rechtsphilosophie oder das Naturrecht*,
fourth edition (Vienna, 1852), p. 64, first French edition (Paris, 1838),
p. 54; and more recently Gunnar Rexius, 'Studien zur Staatslehre der
historischen Schule', *Historische Zeitschrift*, cvii, 1911, Frieda Braun;
Edmund Burke in Deutschland (Heidelberg, 1917); and Klaus Epstein,
The Genesis of German Conservatism (Princeton, 1966).

30 See Peter Stein, *Regulae Iuris* (Edinburgh, 1966), ch. 3.

31 See Paul Vinogradoff, *The Teaching of Sir Henry Maine* (London,
1904), p. 8: 'He [Maine] approached the study of law mainly under
the guidance of the German school of historical jurisprudence which
had formed itself around Savigny and Eichhorn. The special dis-
quisitions of *Ancient Law* on testament, contract, possession, etc.,
leave no doubt as to his close dependence on Savigny's and Puchta's
writings.'

32 On the derivation of social anthropology from the eighteenth- and
nineteenth-century social and legal philosophers see E. E. Evans-
Pritchard, *Social Anthropology* (London, 1915), p. 23; and Max
Gluckman, *Politics, Law and Ritual in Tribal Society* (New York,
1965), p. 17.

33 In addition to such recent studies as J. W. Burrow, *Evolution and
Society: A Study in Victorian Social Theory* (Cambridge, 1966);
Bentley Glass (ed), *Forerunners of Darwin* (Baltimore, 1959); M.
Banton (ed), *Darwinism and the Study of Society* (London, 1961);
Betty J. Meggers (editor for the Anthropological Society of Washing-
ton), *Evolution and Anthropology: A Centennial Appraisal* (Washing-
ton, 1959); and C. C. Gillispie, *Genesis and Geology* (Cambridge,
Mass., 1951), see in particular on David Hume's influence on Charles
Darwin's grandfather, Erasmus Darwin, H. F. Osborn, *From the
Greeks to Darwin*, second edition (New York, 1929), p. 217; F. C.
Haber in Bentley Glass (ed), op. cit., p. 251; on the fact that all three
of the independent discoverers of the theory of evolution, Charles
Darwin, Alfred Russell Wallace and Herbert Spencer, owed the
suggestion to social theory see J. Arthur Thompson, 'Darwin's
predecessors' in A. C. Seward (ed) *Darwin and Modern Science*
(Cambridge, 1909), p. 19; and on Darwin in particular see E. Radl,
Geschichte der biologischen Theorien, II (Leipzig, 1909), p. 121.

See also C. S. Peirce, 'Evolutionary love' (1893), reprinted in his *Collected Papers*, edited by C. Hartshorn and P. Weiss (Cambridge, Mass., 1935), vol 6, p. 293: '*The Origin of Species* of Darwin merely extends politico-economic views of progress to the entire realm of animal and vegetable life.' The whole position has been well summed up by Simon N. Patten, *The Development of English Thought* (New York, 1899), p. xxiii: 'Just as Adam Smith was the last of the moralists and the first of the economists, so Darwin was the last of the economists and the first of the biologists.' Two well-known passages by Sir Frederick Pollock will also bear repetition, the first from *Oxford Lectures and Other Discourses* (London, 1890), p. 41:

> The doctrine of evolution is nothing else than the historical method applied to the facts of nature, the historical method is nothing else than the doctrine of evolution applied to human societies and institutions. When Charles Darwin created the philosophy of natural history (for no less title is due to the idea which transformed the knowledge of organic nature from a multitude of particulars into a continuous whole) he was working in the same spirit and towards the same end as the great publicists who, heeding his field as little as he heeded theirs, had laid in the patient study of historical fact the basis of a solid and rational philosophy of politics and law. Savigny, whom we do not yet know or honour enough, or our own Burke, whom we know and honour, but cannot honour enough, were Darwinians before Darwin. In some measure the same may be said of the great Frenchman Montesquieu, whose unequal but illuminating genius was lost in a generation of formalists.

The second passage is from *Essays in the Law* (London, 1922), p. 11: '*Ancient Law* and *The Origin of Species* were really the outcome, in different branches, of one and the same intellectual movement—that which we associate with the word Evolution.'

The claim to have been Darwinians before Darwin had been made in these words by the linguists August Schleicher, *Die Darwinsche Theorie und die Sprachwissenschaft* (Weimar, 1867), and Max Müller, 'Darwin's Philosophy of Language', *Fraser's Magazine*, vii, 1873, 662.

34 It is indeed to be feared that in social anthropology some of the most enthusiastic advocates of evolutionism, such as the disciples of Leslie A. White, by combining the legitimate 'specific' evolution with what they call 'general' evolution of the sort described above may once more discredit the revived evolutionary approach: see in particular M. D. Sahlins and E. R. Service, *Evolution and Culture* (Ann Arbor, Mich., 1960).

35 See C. H. Waddington, *The Ethical Animal* (London, 1960); T. H. Huxley and Julian Huxley, *Evolution and Ethics 1893–1943* (London,

1947); J. Needham, *Time: The Refreshing River* (London, 1943); and A. G. N. Flew, *Evolutionary Ethics* (London, 1967).

36 Carl Menger, *Problems of Economics and Sociology*, edited by Louis Schneider (Urbana, Ill., 1963), p. 94.

37 At the head of this tradition one should probably mention B. de Spinoza and his often quoted statement in *Ethics* (Everyman edition, p. 187) that, 'He is a free man who lives according to the dictates of reason alone.'

38 Voltaire, *Dictionnaire Philosophique*, s.v. 'Loi', in *Oeuvres complètes de Voltaire*, edited by Hachette, tom. xviii, p. 432: 'Voulez-vous avoir de bonnes lois? Brulez les vôtres et faites nouvelles.'

39 R. A. Palmer, *The Age of Democratic Revolution*, vol. 1 (Princeton, 1959), p. 114.

40 Edmund Burke, 'A vindication of natural society', Preface in *Works* (London, 1808), p. 7.

41 Alexander Herzen, *From the Other Shore*, edited by I. Berlin (London, 1956), pp. 28 and 141.

42 Hans Reichenbach, *The Rise of Scientific Philosophy* (Berkeley, Calif., 1951), p. 141.

43 Quoted in John Maynard Keynes, *Two Memoirs* (London, 1949), p. 97.

44 See J. Piaget, *The Child's Conception of the World* (London, 1929), p. 359: 'The child begins by seeking purpose everywhere and it is only secondarily that it is concerned with classing them as purposes of the things themselves (animism) and purposes of the makers of the things (artificialism).'

45 As, following earlier writers, I have myself done in the past. For the reasons why this expression now appears to me misleading see my lecture on 'Kinds of rationalism' in *S.P.P.E.*

46 See my paper on 'The primacy of the abstract' in A. Koestler and J. R. Smithies (eds), *Beyond Reductionism* (London, 1969).

47 See Gilbert Ryle, *The Concept of Mind* (London, 1949).

48 See G. W. F. Hegel, *Philosophie der Weltgeschichte*, ed G. Lasson, third edition (Leipzig, 1930), and reprinted in *Gesellschaft, Staat, Geschichte*, edited by F. Bülow (Leipzig, no date), p. 317: 'Die Richtung, die an der Abstraktion festhält, ist der *Liberalismus*, über den das Konkrete immer siegt, und gegen das er überall Bankrott macht.' The passage is not contained in the corresponding places of the *Vorlesungen über die Philosophie der Geschichte* in *Werke* (Berlin, 1837), vol 9 or in the *Jubiläumsausgabe* (Stuttgart, 1928), vol. 11, pp. 556–7.

CHAPTER TWO COSMOS AND TAXIS

* Adam Smith, *The Theory of Moral Sentiments* (London, 1759), Part 6, ch. 2, penultimate paragraph. It deserves to be noted that this passage contains some of the basic concepts and terms we shall have to use throughout this book: the conception of a spontaneous order of the *Great Society* as contrasted with a deliberate *arrangement* of the elements; the distinction between *coincidence* and *opposition* between the rules (*principles of motion*) inherent in the elements and those imposed upon them by legislation; and the interpretation of the social process as a *game* which will go on smoothly if the two kinds of rules are in concord but will produce *disorder* if they are in conflict.

1 See my essay on 'The theory of complex phenomena', in F. A. Hayek, *Studies in Philosophy, Politics and Economics* (London and Chicago, 1967, henceforth referred to as *S.P.P.E.*). It was in fact at first entirely the result of methodological considerations that led me to resume the use of the unpopular concept of 'order': see also F. A. Hayek, *The Counter-Revolution of Science* (Chicago, 1952), p. 39: 'If social phenomena showed no order except in so far as they were consciously designed, there would indeed be no room for a theoretical science of society and there would be, as is often maintained, only problems of psychology.' In recent discussion the term 'system' is often used in much the same sense in which I use here 'order', which still seems to me preferable.

2 It would seem that the currency of the concept of order in political theory goes back to St Augustine. See in particular his dialogue *Ordo* in J. P. Migne (ed) *Patrologiae cursus completus sec. lat.* 32/47 (Paris, 1861–2), and in a German version *Die Ordnung*, trans. C. J. Peel, fourth edition (Paderborn, 1966).

3 See L. S. Stebbing, *A Modern Introduction to Logic* (London, 1933), p. 228: 'When we know how a set of elements is ordered, we have a basis for inference.' See also Immanuel Kant, *Werke* (Akademie Ausgabe), *Nachlass*, vol 6, p. 669: 'Ordnung ist die Zusammenfügung nach Regeln.'

4 See E. E. Evans-Pritchard, *Social Anthropology* (London, 1951), p. 49; see also ibid., p. 19:

It is evident that there must be uniformities and regularities in social life, that society must have some sort of order, or its members could not live together. It is only because people know the kind of behaviour expected of them, and what kind of behaviour to expect from others, in the various situations of life, and coordinate their activities in submission to rules and under the guidance of values that each and all are able to go about their affairs. They can make predictions, anticipate events, and lead their lives in harmony with their fellows because every society has a form or pattern which allows us to speak of it as a system, or structure, within which, and in accordance with which, its members live their lives.

5 See L. S. Stebbing, op. cit., p. 229: 'Order is most *apparent* where man has been at work.'

6 See J. Ortega y Gasset, *Mirabeau o el politico* (1927), in *Obras Completas* (Madrid, 1947), vol. 3, p. 603: 'Orden no es una presión que desde fuera se ejerce sobra la sociedad, sin un equilibrio que se suscita en su interior.'

7 See H. von Foerster and G. W. Zopf, Jr (eds) *Principles of Self-Organization* (New York, 1962) and, on the anticipation of the main conceptions of cybernetics by Adam Smith, cf. G. Hardin, *Nature and Man's Fate* (New York, 1961), p. 54; and Dorothy Emmet, *Function, Purpose and Powers* (London, 1958), p. 90.

8 See H. Kuhn, 'Ordnung im Werden und Zerfall', in H. Kuhn and F. Wiedmann (eds), *Das Problem der Ordnung* (Sechster Deutscher Kongress für Philosophie, Munich, 1960, publ. Meisenheim am Glan, 1962), especially p. 17.

9 See Werner Jaeger, *Paideia: The Ideals of Greek Culture*, trans. G. Highet, vol. 1, second edition (New York, 1945), p. 110, about 'Anaximander of Miletus transferring the concept of *diké* from the social life of the city-state to the realm of nature. . . . This is the original of the philosophical idea of cosmos: for the word originally signified the *right order* in a state or in a community'; and ibid., p. 179: 'So the physicist's cosmos became by a curious retrogression in thought, the pattern of eunomia in human society.' See also the same author's 'Praise of law' in P. Sayre (ed), *Interpretations of Modern Legal Philosophies: Essays in Honor of Roscoe Pound* (New York, 1947), especially p. 358:

> A world thus 'justified' could be called rightly by another term taken over from the social order, a cosmos. That word occurs for the first time in the language of the Ionian philosophers; by taking this step and extending the rule of *diké* to reality as a whole they clearly revealed the nature of Greek legal thought and showed that it was based on the relationship of justice to being.

And ibid., p. 361: 'The law on which it [the *polis*] was founded was not a mere decree but the *nomos*, which originally meant the sum total of that which was respected by all living custom with regard to what is right and wrong'; and ibid., p. 365 on the fact that even during the period of the dissolution of the old Greek faith in law: 'the strict relationship of the *nomos* to the nature of the cosmos was not universally questioned.'

For Aristotle, who connects *nomos* with *taxis* rather than *kosmos* (see *Politics*, 1287a, 18, and especially 1326a, 30: *ho te gar nomos taxis tis esti*), it is characteristically inconceivable that the order resulting from the *nomos* should exceed what the orderer can survey, 'for who will command its over-swollen multitude in war? or who will serve as its herald, unless he had the lungs of Stentor?' The creation of order in such a multitude is for him a task only the gods can achieve. Elsewhere (*Ethics*, IX, x, §3) he even argues that a state, i.e. an ordered society, of a hundred thousand people is impossible.

10 Adam Smith, *Wealth of Nations*, edited by E. Cannan, vol. 1, p. 421.

11 See G. Sartori, *Democratic Theory* (Detroit, 1962), p. 306:

> Western man for two and a half millennia has sought liberty in the law. . . . [Yet] the widespread scepticism about the value of the juridical protection of liberty is not unjustified. The reason for this is that our conception of law has changed; and that, as a consequence, law can no longer give us the protection that it did give us in the past.

12 See Philo of Alexandria, *Quod omnis probus liber sit*, 452, 45, Loeb edition, vol. IX, p. 36: '*hosoi de meta nomou zosin, eleuteroi*'. On freedom in ancient Greece see in particular Max Pohlenz, *The Idea of Freedom in Greek Life and Thought* (Dordrecht, 1962). On Cicero and the Roman concept of liberty generally see U. von Lübtow, *Blüte und Verfall der römischen Freiheit* (Berlin, 1953); Theo Mayer-Maly, 'Rechtsgeschichte der Freiheitsidee in Antike und Mittelalter', *Österreichische Zeitschrift für öffentliches Recht*, N.F. VI, 1956; and G. Crifo, 'Su alcuni aspetti della libertà in Roma', *Archivio Giuridico 'Filippo Serafini'*, sesta serie, xxiii, 1958.

13 See R. W. Southern, *The Making of the Middle Ages* (New Haven, 1953), p. 107 *et seq.*:

> The hatred of that which was governed, not by rule, but by will, went very deep in the Middle Ages. . . . The higher one rose towards liberty, the more the area of action was covered by law, the less it was subject by will. . . . Law was not the enemy of freedom; on the contrary, the outline of liberty was traced by the bewildering variety of law which was slowly evolved during our period. . . . High and low alike sought liberty by insisting on enlarging the number of rules under which they lived. . . . It was only when the quality of freedom was articulated by being attached to the status of knight, burgess or baron that it could be observed, analysed and measured. . . . Liberty is a creation of law, and law is reason in action; it is reason which makes men, as we should say, ends in themselves. Tyranny, whether of King John or of the Devil, is a manifestation of the absence of law.

14 Most emphatically, perhaps, Adam Ferguson, *Principles of Moral and Political Science* (Edinburgh, 1792), vol. 2, p. 258 *et seq.*:

> Liberty or freedom is not, as the origin of the name may seem to imply, an exemption from all restraint, but rather the most

effectual application of every just restraint to all the members of a
free state, whether they be magistrates or subjects.

It is under just restraints only that every person is safe, and
cannot be invaded, either in the freedom of his person, his
property, or innocent action. . . . The establishment of a just
and effectual government is of all circumstances in civil society
the most essential to freedom: that everyone is justly said to be
free in proportion as the government under which he resides is
sufficiently powerful to protect him, at the same time that it is
sufficiently restrained and limited to prevent the abuse of this
power.

15 Daniel Webster is credited with the statement that 'Liberty is the
creature of law, essentially different from the authorized licentious-
ness that trespasses on right'; and Charles Evans Hughes with that
'Liberty and Law are one and inseparable'. There are many
similar statements by continental legal scholars of the last century,
e.g. Charles Beudant, *Le Droit individuel et l'état* (Paris, 1891), p. 5:
'Le Droit, au sens le plus général du mot, est la science de la liberté';
and Karl Binding who argued somewhere that 'Das Recht ist eine
Ordnung menschlicher Freiheit.'

16 See J. Bentham, 'Principles of the civil code', in *Theory of Legislation*, edited by C. K. Ogden (London, 1931), p. 98: 'Laws cannot be
made except at the expense of liberty.' Also in *Deontology* (London
and Edinburgh, 1834), vol. 2, p. 59:

There are few words which, with its derivations, have been more
mischievous than this word liberty. When it means anything
beyond mere caprice and dogmatism, it means good government;
and if good government had had the good fortune to occupy the
same place in the public mind which has been occupied by
liberty, the crimes and follies which have disgraced and retarded
the progress of political improvement would hardly have been
committed. The usual definition of liberty—that it is the right to
do everything that the law does not forbid—shows with what
carelessness words are used in ordinary discourse or composition;
for if the laws are bad, what becomes of liberty? and if the laws are
good, where is its value? Good laws have a definite intelligible
meaning; they pursue an evidently useful end by obviously
appropriate means.

17 See for example, Jean Salvaire, *Autorité et liberté* (Montpellier, 1932),
p. 65 *et seq.*, who argues that 'the complete realization of liberty is,
in fact, nothing else but the complete abolition of law. . . . Law and
liberty are mutually exclusive'.

18 Edmund Burke, 'Letter to W. Elliot' (1795), in *Works* (London, 1808),
vol. 7, p. 366:

These analogies between bodies natural and politick, though
they may sometimes illustrate arguments, furnish no arguments
for themselves. They are but too often used under the colour of a
specious philosophy, to find apologies for the despair of laziness
and pusillanimity, and to excuse the want of all manly efforts,
when the exigencies of our country call for them the more loudly.

19 For a characteristic use of the contrast between 'organism' and
'organization' see Adolf Wagner, *Grundlegung der politischen Ökonomie*,
I. Grundlagen der Volkswirtschaft (Leipzig, 1876), § § 149 and 299.

20 See Immanuel Kant, *Kritik der Urteilskraft* (Berlin, 1790), Part 2,
section 1, § 65n.: 'So hat man sich bei einer neuerlich unternommenen
gänzlichen Umbildung eines grossen Volkes zu einem Staat des
Wortes *Organisation* häufig für Einrichtung der Magistraturen usw.
und selbst des ganzen Staatskörpers sehr schicklich bedient.'

21 See H. Balzac, *Autre étude de femme*, in *La Comédie Humaine*, Pleiade
edition, vol. 3, p. 226: 'Organiser, par example, est un mot de l'Empire
et qui contient Napoléon tout entier.'

22 See, for example, the journal edited by H. de Saint Simon and Auguste
Comte called *Organisateur*, reprinted in *Oeuvres de Saint Simon et
d'Enfantin* (Paris, 1865–78), vol. 20, especially p. 220, where the aim
of the work is described as 'D'imprimer au XIX siècle le caractère
organisateur'.

23 See in particular Louis Blanc, *Organisation du travail* (Paris, 1839),
and H. Ahrens, *Rechtsphilosophie*, fourth edition (Vienna, 1852) on
'organization' as the magic word of the communists and socialists;
see also Francis Lieber, 'Anglican and Gallican liberty' (1848), in
Miscellaneous Writings (Philadelphia, 1881), vol 2, p. 385:

> The fact that Gallican liberty expects everything from *organization*,
> while Anglican liberty inclines to development, explains why
> we see in France so little improvement and expansion of
> institutions; but when improvements are attempted, a total aboli-
> tion of the preceding state of things—a beginning *ab ovo*—a
> rediscussion of the first elementary principles.

24 See Ernest Renan, *L'Avenir de la Science* (1890), in *Oeuvres complètes*
(Paris, 1949), vol. 3, p. 757: 'ORGANISER SCIENTIFIQUEMENT L'HUMAN-
ITÉ, tel est donc le dernier mot de la science moderne, telle est son
audacieuse mais légitime prétention.'

25 See *Shorter Oxford Dictionary*, s.v. 'organization', which shows,
however, that the term was already used by John Locke.

26 Jean Labadie (ed), *L'Allemagne, a-t-elle le secret de l'organisation?*
(Paris, 1916).

27 See Dwight Waldo, 'Organization theory: an elephantine problem',
Public Administration Review, xxx, 1961, and reprinted in *General*

Systems, Yearbook of the Society for General System Research, VII 1962, the preceding volume of which contains a useful collection of, articles on the theory of organization.

CHAPTER THREE   PRINCIPLES AND EXPEDIENCY

* The Constitution of the State of North Carolina. The idea is probably derived from David Humes's, *Essays,* in *Works* III, p. 482: 'A government, says Machiavelli, must often be brought back to its original principles.' An earlier version of this chapter appeared in *Towards Liberty, Essays in Honor of Ludwig von Mises* (Menlo Park, Calif., 1971), vol. 1.

1 See F. A. Hayek, *The Constitution of Liberty* (London and Chicago, 1960).

2 Adam Smith, *Wealth of Nations,* edited by E. Cannan (London, 1930), vol. 2, p. 184; see also John Locke, *Second Treatise on Government,* edited by P. Laslett (Cambridge, 1960), section 22: 'a liberty to follow my own will in all things, where the rules prescribe not.'

3 See A. V. Dicey, *Lectures on the Relation between Law and Public Opinion during the Nineteenth Century* (London, 1914), p. 257:

> The beneficial effect of State intervention, especially in the form of legislation, is direct, immediate, and so to speak visible, whilst its evil effects are gradual and indirect, and lie outside our sight. . . . Hence the majority of mankind must almost of necessity look with undue favour upon government intervention. This natural bias can be counteracted only by the existence, in a given society, . . . of a presumption or prejudice in favour of individual liberty, that is of *laissez-faire.*

Similarly, E. Küng, *Der Interventionismus* (Bern, 1941), p. 360: 'Die günstigen und gewollten Nachwirkungen der meisten wirtschaftspolitischen Massnahmen treten kurz nach ihrer Inkraftsetzung auf, die manchmal schwerer wirkenden Fernwirkungen erst später.'

4 As has been preached with such far-reaching effect on the American intellectuals by John Dewey: see for example, his essay 'Force and coercion', *International Journal of Ethics,* xvi, 1916, especially p. 362. 'Whether the use of force is justified or not . . . is, in substance, a question of efficiency (including economy) of means in the accomplishment of ends.'

5 Benjamin Constant, 'De l'arbitraire', in *Oeuvres politiques,* edited by C. Louandre (Paris, 1874), pp. 71–2.

6 Frederic Bastiat, *Ce qu'on voit et ce qu'on ne voit pas en economie politique* (Paris, 1850), English translation in his *Selected Essays in Political Economy,* edited by G. B. de Huszar (Princeton, 1964), his last and most brilliant essay.

7 Carl Menger, *Problems of Economics and Sociology*, edited by L. Schneider (Urbana, Ill., 1963).

8 See W. Y. Elliott, *The Pragmatic Revolt in Politics* (New York, 1928).

9 On these lines particularly R. A. Dahl and Charles Lindblom, *Politics, Economics, and Welfare* (New York, 1953), pp. 3-18, e.g. p. 16: 'Techniques and not "isms" are the kernel of rational action in the Western world. Both socialism and capitalism are dead.' This is precisely the cause of our drift.

10 London and Chicago, 1944.

11 See Preface to W. S. Jevons, *The State in Relation to Labour* (London, 1882).

12 Herbert Spencer, *Justice: Being Part IV of the Principles of Ethics* (London, 1891), p. 44.

13 J. A. Schumpeter, *History of Economic Analysis* (New York, 1954), p. 394.

14 Adam Smith, *op. cit.* vol. 1, p. 435.

15 See for example, Max Weber, *On Law in Economy and Society*, edited by Max Rheinstein (Cambridge, Mass., 1954), p. 298.

16 See the essays on *Capitalism and the Historians*, by various authors, edited by the present writer (London and Chicago, 1953).

17 David Hume, *Essays*, in *Works* III, p. 125, and compare the passages by J. S. Mill and Lord Keynes quoted on p. 113 and in note 14 to ch. 6 of my book, *The Constitution of Liberty*, to which may now be added a similar statement by G. Mazzini which I have seen quoted without source: 'Ideas rule the world and its events. A revolution is the passage of an idea from theory to practice. Whatever men say, material interests never have caused, and never will cause a revolution.'

18 It was therefore also not, as J. A. Schumpeter kindly suggested in a review of *The Road to Serfdom* in *Journal of Political Economy*, xiv, 1946, 'politeness to a fault' but profound conviction about what are the decisive factors if that book 'hardly ever attributes to opponents anything beyond intellectual error'.

19 As one of Carl Schmitt's followers, George Dahm, reviewing Schmitt's *Drei Arten des rechtswissenschaftlichen Denkens* (Hamburg, 1934), in *Zeitschrift für die gesamte Staatswissenschaft*, xcv, 1935, p. 181, wrote, all Schmitt's works 'sind von Anfang an auf ein bestimmtes Ziel gerichtet gewesen: die Entlarvung und Zerstörung des liberalen Rechtsstaates und die Überwindung des Gesetzgebungsstaates'. The most appropriate comment on Schmitt came from Johannes Huizinga, *Homo Ludens* (1944), English translation (London, 1947), p. 209:

> I know of no sadder and deeper fall from human reason than Schmitt's barbarous and pathetic delusion about the friend-foe principle. His inhuman cerebrations do not even hold water as a piece of formal logic. For it is not war that is serious but peace.

. . . Only by transcending this pitiable friend-foe relationship will mankind enter into the dignity of man's estate. Schmitt's brand of 'seriousness' merely takes us back to the savage level.

20 See Carl Schmitt, op. cit., p. 11 *et seq.*

CHAPTER FOUR   THE CHANGING CONCEPT OF LAW

* Julius Paulus, Roman jurist of the third century A.D., in *Digests* 50.17.1: 'What is right is not derived from the rule but the rule arises from our knowledge of what is right.' See also the observation by the twelfth-century glossator Franciscus Accursius, gloss to *Digests*, I.1.1. pr. 9: 'est autem ius a iustitia, sicut a matre sua, ergo prius fuit iustitia quam ius.' On the whole complex of problems to be discussed in this chapter see Peter Stein, *Regulae Iuris* (Edinburgh, 1966), especially p. 20: 'in origin *lex* was declaratory of *ius*.'

1 Bernhard Rehfeld, *Die Wurzeln des Rechts* (Berlin, 1951), p. 67:

> Das Auftauchen des Phänomens der Gesetzgebung . . . bedeutet in der Menschheitsgeschichte die Erfindung der Kunst, Recht und Unrecht zu *machen*. Bis dahin hatte man geglaubt, Recht nicht setzen, sondern nur anwenden zu können als etwas, das seit jeher war. An dieser Vorstellung gemessen ist die Erfindung der Gesetzgebung vielleicht die folgenschwerste gewesen, die je gemacht wurde—folgenschwerer als die des Feuers oder des Schiesspulvers—denn am stärksten von allen hat sie das Schicksal des Menschen in seine Hand gelegt.

2 This illusion, characteristic of many thinkers of our time, was expressed by Lord Keynes in a letter to me on 28 June 1944, quoted in R. F. Harrod, *The Life of John Maynard Keynes* (London, 1951), p. 436, in which, commenting on my book *The Road to Serfdom*, he remarked that 'dangerous acts can be done safely in a community which thinks and feels rightly, which would be the way to hell if they were executed by those who think and feel wrongly'.

3 David Hume, *Treatise* II, p. 306:

> But, though it be possible for men to maintain a small unculti- vated society without government, it is impossible they should maintain a society of any kind without justice, and the observance of the three fundamental laws concerning the stability of possession, translation by consent, and the performance of promises. They are therefore antecedent to government.

See also Adam Ferguson, *Principles of Moral and Political Science* (Edinburgh, 1792), vol. 1, p. 262:

The first object of concert and convention, on the part of man,
is not to give society existence, but to perfect the society in which
he finds himself already by nature placed; not to establish
subordination, but to correct the abuse of subordination already
established: And that material, on which the political genius of
men is to work, is not, as poets have figured, a scattered race, in a
state of individuality to be collected together into troops, by
the charms of music or the lessons of philosophy. But a material
much nearer to the point to which the political act would carry
it, a troop of men by mere instinct assembled together; placed
in the subordinate relation of parent and child, of noble and
plebeian, if not of rich and poor, or other adventitious, if not
original distinction, which constitutes, in fact, a relation of power
and dependence, by which a few are in condition to govern the
many, and a part has an ascendance over the whole;

and Carl Menger, *Problems of Economics and Sociology* (Urbana, Ill.,
1963), especially p. 227:

National law in its most original form is thus, to be sure, not the
result of a contract or of reflection aiming at the assurance of
common welfare. Nor is it, indeed, given with the nation, as
the historical school asserts. Rather, it is older than the appearance
of the latter. Indeed, it is one of the strongest ties by which the
population of a territory becomes a nation and achieves state
organization.

4 See Gilbert Ryle, 'Knowing how and knowing that', *Proceedings of
the Aristotelian Society*, 1945–6, and *The Concept of Mind* (London,
1949), ch. 2; see also my essay 'Rules, perception and intelligibility',
Proceedings of the British Academy, xlviii, 1962, reprinted in my
Studies in Philosophy, Politics and Economics (London and Chicago,
1967) (*S.P.P.E.*).
5 See Sten Gagnèr, *Studien zur Ideengeschichte der Gesetzgebung*
(Uppsala, 1960); Alan Gewirt, *Marsilius of Padua, Defender of Peace*
(New York, 1951 and 1956); and T. F. T. Plucknett, *Statutes and their
Interpretation in the First Half of the Fourteenth Century* (Cambridge,
1922).
6 See my essay on 'Notes on the evolution of rules of conduct', in
S.P.P.E.
7 The best documented and most fully studied instance of the development of distinct 'cultural' traditions among separated groups of
animals of the same species is that of the Japanese macaque monkeys
which in comparatively recent times were split by the extension of human cultivation into distinct groups which appear in a short time to
have acquired clearly distinguishable cultural traits. See also on this

J. E. Frisch, 'Research on primate behaviour in Japan', *American Anthropologist*, lxi, 1959; F. Imanishi, 'Social behavior in Japanese monkeys: "Macaca fuscata",' *Psychologia*, I. 1957; and S. Kawamura, 'The process of sub-cultural propagation among Japanese macaques,' in C. H. Southwick (ed), *Primate Social Behavior* (Princeton, 1963).

8 V. C. Wynne-Edwards, *Animal Dispersion in Relation to Social Behaviour* (Edinburgh, 1966), p. 456; see also ibid., p. 12:

> The substitution of a parcel of ground as the object of competition in place of the actual food it contains so that each individual or family unit has a separate holding of the resource to exploit, is the simplest and most direct kind of limiting convention it is possible to have. . . . Much space is devoted in later chapters to studying the almost endless variety of density limiting factors . . . The food territory just considered is concrete enough. . . . We shall find that abstract goals are especially characteristic of gregarious species.

And ibid., p. 190:

> 'There is little new in this situation so far as mankind is concerned, except in degree of complexity; all conventional behaviour is inherently social and moral in character; and so far from being an exclusively human attribute, we find that the primary code of conventions evolved to prevent population density from exceeding the optimum, stems not only from the lowest vertebrate classes, but appears well established among the invertebrate phyla as well.

9 David Lack, *The Life of the Robin*, revised edition (London, 1946), p. 35.

10 Apart from the well-known works of Konrad Z. Lorenz and N. Tinbergen see I. Eibl-Eibesfeldt, *Grundlagen der vergleichenden Verhaltensforschung—Ethologie* (Munich, 1967); and Robert Ardrey, *The Territorial Imperative* (New York, 1966).

11 See J. Rawls, 'Justice as fairness', *Philosophical Review*, lxvii, 195.

12 See for example, the description in Konrad Z. Lorenz, *King Solomon's Ring* (London and New York, 1952), p. 188, quoted later in this chapter.

13 See my essay on 'The primacy of the abstract', in A. Koestler and J. R. Smithies (eds) *Beyond Reductionism: New Perspectives in the Life Sciences* (London, 1969).

14 See the works of Noam Chomsky, especially *Current Issues in Linguistic Theory* (The Hague, 1966); and Kenneth L. Pike, *Language in Relation to a Unified Theory of the Structure of Human Behaviour* (The Hague, 1967).

15 See Michael Polanyi, *Personal Knowledge* (London and Chicago, 1958), especially chs. 5 and 6 on 'Skills' and 'Articulation' and my essay on 'Rules, perception and intelligibility' in *S.P.P.E.*

16 Perhaps it should be explicitly pointed out that the distinction between articulated and not-articulated rules is not the same as the more
familiar one between written and unwritten law—neither in the literal
sense of these terms nor in the sense in which statute law is sometimes
described as written law in contrast to the common law. Unwritten
law that is orally handed down may be fully articulated and often was.
Yet a system like that of the common law permits a taking into account of yet unarticulated rules which will often be stated in words for
the first time by a judge expressing what he rightly regards as existing
law.

17 Konrad Z. Lorenz, op. cit., p. 188.

18 See my lecture on *Die Irrtümer des Konstruktivismus und die Grundlagen legitimer Kritik gesellschaftlicher Gebilde* (Munich and Salzburg,
1970), pp. 24 *et seq.*

19 See S. N. Kramer, *History Begins at Sumer* (New York, 1952), p. 52.

20 This did not of course, prevent these men coming later to be regarded as the makers of that law because they had codified it. See
John Burnet, 'Law and nature in Greek ethics', *International Journal
of Ethics*, vii, 1897, p. 332:

> But a code of law framed by a known law-giver, a Zalenkos or a
> Charondas, a Lykurgus or a Solon, could not be accepted in this
> way as part of the everlasting order of things. It was clearly
> 'made', and, therefore, from the point of view of φύσις, artificial
> and arbitrary. It seemed as if it might just as well have been made
> otherwise or not at all. A generation which had seen laws in the
> making could hardly help asking whether all morality had not
> been 'made' in the same way.

21 A. H. M. Jones, *Athenian Democracy* (Oxford, 1957), p. 52.

22 See Lord Acton, *History of Freedom* (London, 1907), p. 12:

> On a memorable occasion the assembled Athenians declared it
> monstrous that they should be prevented from doing whatever
> they chose; no force that existed could restrain them, and they
> resolved that no duty should restrain them, and that they would
> be bound by no laws that were not of their own making. In this
> way the emancipated people of Athens became a tyrant.

23 Aristotle, *Politics*, IV, iv, 4, 1292a, Loeb edition, p. 305:

> And it would seem a reasonable criticism to say that such a
> democracy is not a constitution at all; for where the laws do not
> govern there is no constitution, as the law ought to govern all
> things while the magistrates control particulars, and we ought to
> judge this constitutional government; if then democracy really is
> one of the forms of constitution, it is manifest that an organization

of this kind, in which all things are administered by resolutions of the assembly, is not even a democracy in the proper sense, for it is impossible for a voted resolution to be a universal rule.

24 Max Kaser, *Römische Rechtsgeschichte* (Göttingen, 1950), p. 54.
25 Ibid. See also Max Rheinstein, 'Process and change in the cultural spectrum coincident with expansion: government and law', in C. H. Kraeling and R. M. Adams (eds), *City Invincible* (Chicago, 1960), p. 117:

> The notion that valid norms of conduct might be established by way of legislation was peculiar to later states of Greek and Roman history; in Western Europe it was dormant until the discovery of Roman law and the rise of absolute monarchy. The proposition that all law is the command of a sovereign is a postulate engendered by the democratic ideology of the French Revolution that all law had to emanate from the duly elected representatives of the people. It is not, however, a true description of reality, least of all in the countries of the Anglo-Saxon Common Law.

On Rome in particular see Theodor Mommsen, *Abriss des römischen Staatsrechts* (Leipzig, 1893), p. 319: 'Aber auch mit Hinzuziehung der Bürgerschaft hat der Magistrat der bestehenden Rechtsordnung gegenüber keineswegs freie Hand. Im Gegenteil gilt diese, als nicht durch die Comitien geschaffen, auch nicht als von ihrem Belieben abhängig, vielmehr als ewig und unveränderlich.'
26 Peter Stein, op. cit., p. 20: 'The Romans did not resort readily to legislation in matters of private law.'
27 See W. W. Buckland and A. D. McNair, *Roman Law and Common Law* (Cambridge, 1936).
28 In addition to the authors quoted in F. A. Hayek, *The Constitution of Liberty*, (London and Chicago, 1960), p. 163 and notes 5 and 6, see R. Sohm, *Fränkische Reichs- und Gerichtsverfassung* (Weimar, 1871), p. 102: 'Das Volksrecht ist *das* Recht des deutschen Rechts. Das Volksrecht ist das Stammesgewohnheitsrecht. Die gesetzgebende Gewalt ist in der Staatsgewalt nicht enthalten. Die capitula sind nicht Rechtsnormen, sondern Norm für die Ausübung der königlichen Gewalt'; J. E. A. Jolliffe, *The Constitutional History of Medieval England from the English Settlement to 1485*, second edition (London, 1947), p. 334:

> Until well into the thirteenth century the primitive conception of a society living within the frame of an inherited law had deprived the king of the quality of law-maker and restricted the *commune consilium* to recognition of custom, and participation in adjustments of right and procedure by way of assize. Vital changes

were, no doubt, made, but they were made in such a way as to obscure their real nature as legislative change.

A footnote to this passage points out that Bracton regarded as permissible only *legem in melius convertire* but not *legem mutare*. A similar conclusion may be found in F. Fichtenau, *Arenga, Spätantike und Mittelalter im Spiegel von Urkundenformeln* (Graz and Cologne, 1957), p. 178: 'Früher war dem Herrscher allein das leges custodire aufgegeben gewesen. Recht und Gesetz standen ja über ihm und das Neue musste stets im Alten seine Begründung finden.'

29 Fritz Kern, *Kingship and Law in the Middle Ages*, trans. S. B. Chrimes (London, 1939), p. 151; G. Barraclough, *Law Quarterly Review*, lvi, 1940, p. 76, describes this work as 'two remarkable essays whose conclusions, though they may be modified or limited, will assuredly never be challenged.'

30 See in particular Sten Gagnèr, op. cit.

31 I believe this passage, for which I have lost the reference, is by F. W. Maitland. See also A. V. Dicey, *Law of the Constitution*, ninth edition (London, 1939), p. 370:

> A lawyer, who regards the matter from an exclusively legal point of view, is tempted to assert that the real subject in dispute between statesmen such as Bacon and Wentworth on the one hand, and Coke or Eliot on the other, was whether a strong administration of the Continental type should, or should not, be permanently established in England.

32 See W. S. Holdsworth, *A History of English Law*, vol. 5 (London, 1924), p. 439:

> It was in Coke's writings that this [conception of the supremacy of the common law] and other mediaeval conceptions were given their modern form; and therefore it is largely owing to the influence of his writings that these mediaeval conceptions have become part of our modern law. If their influence upon some parts of our modern law has not been wholly satisfactory, let us remember that they saved Englishmen from a criminal procedure allowed to use torture, and that they preserve for England and the world the constitutional doctrine of the rule of law.

33 Quoted by W. S. Holdsworth, *Some Lessons from Legal History* (London, 1928), p. 18.

34 See David Hume, *Essays* (London, 1875), vol. 2, p. 274:

> All the laws of nature, which regulate property, as well as civil laws, are general, and regard only some essential circumstances of the case, without taking into consideration the characters,

situations, and connexions of the persons concerned, or any particular consequences which may result from the determination of these laws, in any particular case which offers. They deprive, without scruple, a beneficent man of all his possessions, if acquired by mistake, without a good title; in order to bestow them on a selfish miser who has already heaped up immense stores of superfluous riches. Public utility requires that property should be regulated by general inflexible rules; and though such rules are adopted as best serve the same end of public utility, it is impossible for them to prevent all particular hardships, or make beneficial consequences result from every individual case. It is sufficient if the whole plan or scheme be necessary to the support of civil society, and if the balance of good, in the main, do thereby preponderate much above that of evil.

35 The case for relying even in modern times for the development of law on the gradual process of judicial precedent and scholarly interpretation has been persuasively argued by the late Bruno Leoni, *Liberty and the Law* (Princeton, 1961). But although his argument is an effective antidote to the prevailing orthodoxy which believes that only legislation can or ought to alter the law, it has not convinced me that we can dispense with legislation even in the field of private law with which he is chiefly concerned.

36 See W. S. Jevons, *The State in Relation to Labour* (London, 1882), p. 33: 'The great lesson we learn [from 650 years of legislation of English Parliaments] is that legislation with regard to labour has almost always been class-legislation. It is the effort of some dominant body to keep down a lower class, which had begun to show inconvenient aspirations.'

37 H. Kelsen, *What is Justice?* (Berkeley, Calif., 1957), p. 21.

38 F. W. Maitland, *Constitutional History of England* (Cambridge, 1908), p. 382.

39 See David Hume, op. cit., vol. i., p. 125: 'Though men be much governed by interest, yet even interest itself, and all human affairs, are entirely governed by opinion.'

CHAPTER FIVE   NOMOS: THE LAW OF LIBERTY

＊Strabo, *Geography*, 10,4,16, in the Loeb edition by H. L. Jones vol. 5, p. 145. While Strabo lived at the beginning of our era, Ephorus of Kyme whom he quotes and of whose works only fragments are preserved lived from about 400–330 B.C.

1 See for example, the statement by the grammarian Servius of the fourth century A.D. (quoted by P. Stein, *Regulae Iuris*, (Edinburgh, 1966), p. 109): 'ius generale est, sed lex est species, ius ad non scrip-

tum pertinet, leges ad ius scriptum.' It has been suggested with some justification (by Alvaro d'Ors, *De la Guerra, de la Paz* (Madrid, 1954), p. 160, quoted by Carl Schmitt. *Verfassungsrechtliche Aufsätze* (Berlin, 1958), p. 427), that it was a major misfortune that Cicero translated the Greek term *nomos* with *lex* instead of with *ius*. For Cicero's use of the term *lex* see in particular *De legibus*, II, v–vi, Loeb edition by C. W. Keyes (London, 1929), pp. 384–6: 'Est lex iustorum iniustorumque distinctio . . . nec vero iam aliam esse ullam legem puto non modo habendam, sed ne appellandum quidem.'

2 See the often quoted statement by H. Triepel in *Festgabe der Berliner juristischen Fakultät für W. Kahl* (Tübingen, 1923), p. 93: 'Heilig ist nicht das Gesetz, heilig ist nur das Recht, und das Recht steht über dem Gesetz.'

3 See the passages from David Hume, Adam Ferguson and Carl Menger quoted in chapter 4, note 3, of this book.

4 See H. L. A. Hart, *The Concept of Law* (Oxford, 1961).

5 See James Coolidge Carter, *Law, Its Origin, Growth and Function* (New York and London, 1907), p. 59: 'All complaints by one man against another, whether of a civil or criminal nature, arose from the fact that something had been done *contrary to the complainant's expectations of what should have been done.*' See also ibid., p. 331:

> The great general rule governing human action at the beginning, namely that it must conform to fair expectations, is still the scientific rule. All the forms of conduct complying with this rule are consistent with each other and become the recognized customs. All those inconsistent with it are stigmatized as bad practices. The body of custom therefore tends to become a harmonious system.

On this important work which is not as well known as it deserves see M. J. Gronson, 'The juridical evolutionism of James Coolidge Carter', *University of Toronto Law Journal*, 1953.

6 Roscoe Pound, *Jurisprudence*, vol. 1 (New York, 1959), p. 371.

7 As we frequently have to speak of 'a group prevailing over others' it should perhaps be stressed that this does not necessarily mean victory in a clash of forces, or even that the members of such a group will displace the individual members of other groups. It is much more likely that the success of a group will attract members of others which thus become incorporated in the first. Sometimes the successful group will become an aristocracy within a given society and as a result the rest will model their conduct after that of the former. But in all these instances the members of the more successful group will often not know to which peculiarity they owe their success, nor cultivate that trait because they know what depends on it.

8 Many of the earlier theorists of natural law had come close to an

insight into this relation between the rules of law and the order of actions which it serves. See Roscoe Pound, *Interpretations of Legal History* (New York, 1923), p. 5:

> In fact jurist or text-writer or judge or legislator, working
> under the theory of natural law, measured all situations and sought
> to solve all difficulties by referring them to an idealized picture
> of the social order of the time and place and a conception of the
> aims of law in terms of that order. . . . Accordingly the ideal of
> the social order was taken to be the ultimate reality of which
> legal institutions and rules and doctrines were but reflections or
> declarations.

The medieval conception of a social order was, however, still largely one of the particular status of the different individuals or classes and only some of the late Spanish schoolmen approached the conception of an abstract order based on a uniform law for all.

9 For the use of this term by the late Spanish schoolmen see C. von Kaltenborn, *Die Vorläufer des Hugo Grotius* (Leipzig, 1848), p. 146. The conception of justice being confined to action towards others however, goes back at least to Aristotle, *Nicomachean Ethics*, V, i, 15–20, Loeb edition, pp. 256–9.

10 This is a legitimate objection to the manner in which I have treated the subject in *The Constitution of Liberty* (London and Chicago, 1960) and I hope that the present statement will satisfy the critics who have pointed out this defect, such as Lord Robbins (*Economica*, February, 1961), J. C. Rees (*Philosophy*, 38, 1963) and R. Hamowy (*The New Individualist Review*, 1 (1), 1961).

11 This is, of course, implied in Immanuel Kant's (and Herbert Spencer's) formula about the 'equal liberty of others' being the only legitimate ground for a restriction of liberty by law. On the whole subject see John Rawls, *A Theory of Justice* (Oxford, 1972).

12 See P. A. Freund, 'Social justice and the law', in R. B. Brandt (ed), *Social Justice* (New York, 1962), p. 96: 'Reasonable expectations are more generally the ground rather than the product of law'.

13 Heinrich Dernburg, *Pandekten*, second edition (Berlin, 1888), p. 85: 'Die Lebensverhältnisse tragen, wenn auch mehr oder weniger entwickelt, ihr Mass und ihre Ordnung in sich. Diese den *Dingen innewohnende Ordnung* nennt man Natur der Sache. Auf sie muss der denkende Jurist zurückgehen, wo es an einer positiven Norm fehlt oder wenn dieselbe unvollständig oder unklar ist.'

14 See O. W. Holmes, Jr, *The Common Law* (New York, 1963), p. 7:

> The life of law has not been logic, it has been experience. The felt
> necessities of the time, the prevalent moral and political theories,
> institutions of public policy, avowed or unconscious, even the

prejudices which judges share with their fellow-men, have a good deal more to do than syllogisms in determining the rules by which men should be governed. The law embodies the story of a nation's development through many centuries, and it cannot be dealt with as if it contained only the axioms and corollaries of a book of mathematics.

See also Roscoe Pound, *Law and Morals* (Chapel Hill, N.C., 1926), p. 97: 'The problem of law is to keep conscious free-willing beings from interference with each other. It is so to order them that each shall exercise his freedom in a way consistent with the freedom of all others, since all others are to be regarded equally as ends in themselves.'

15 Paul Van der Eycken, *Méthode positive de l'interprétation juridique* (Brussels and Paris, 1907), p. 401:

On regardait précédemment le droit comme le produit de la volonté consciente du législateur. Aujourd'hui on voit en lui une force naturelle. Mais si l'on peut attribuer au droit l'épithète de naturel, c'est, nous l'avons dit, dans un sens bien différent de celui qu'avait autrefois l'expression de 'droit naturel'. Elle signifiait alors que la nature avait imprimé en nous, comme un élément même de la raison, certains principes dont la foule des articles des codes n'étaient que les applications. La même expression doit signifier actuellement que le droit résulte des relations de fait entre les choses. Comme ces relations elles-mêmes, le droit naturel est en travail perpetuel. . . . Le législateur n'a de ce droit qu'une conscience fragmentaire; il la traduit par les prescriptions qu'il edicte. Lorsqu'il s'agira de fixer le sens de celle-ci, où faudra-t-il le chercher? Manifestement à leur source: c'est-à-dire dans les exigences de la vie sociale. La probabilité la plus forte de découvrir le sens de la loi se trouve là. De même lorsqu'il s'agira de combler les lacunes de la loi, ce n'est pas aux déductions logiques, c'est aux nécessités qu'on demandera la solution.

16 C. Perelman and L. Olbrechts-Tyteca, *La Nouvelle Rhétorique— traité de l'argumentation* (Paris, 1958), vol. 1, pp. 264–70, especially §46: *Contradiction et Incompatibilité* and §47: *Procédés permettant d'éviter un incompatibilité*, of which only a few significant passages can be quoted here. p. 263:

L'incompatibilité dépend soit de la nature des choses, soit d'une décision humaine.' (p. 264.) 'Des incompatibilités peuvent résulter de l'application à des situations determinés de plusieurs règles morales ou juridiques, de textes legaux ou sacrés. Alors que la contradiction entre deux propositions suppose un formalisme où du moins une système des notions univoques, l'incompatibilité est toujours relative à des circonstances contingentes, que celles-ci soient constituées par des lois naturelles, des événements particuliers où des décisions humaines.

Similarly see also Charles P. Curtis, 'A better theory of legal interpretation', *Vanderbilt Law Review*, iii, 1949, p. 423: 'The most important criterion is simply consistency with all the rest of the law. This contract or that will is a very small part of our total law, just as truly as this or that statute is a larger piece; and, though Justice has larger aims, the virtue on which the Law stakes its hopes is consistency.'

17 See Jürgen von Kempski, 'Bemerkungen zum Begriff der Gerechtigkeit', *Studium Generale*, xii, 1959, and reprinted in the same author's *Recht und Politik* (Stuttgart, 1965), p. 51: 'Wir wollen davon sprechen, dass den Privatrechtsordnungen ein Verträglichkeitsprinzip für Handlungen zu Grunde liegt'; and the same author's *Grundlagen zu einer Strukturtheorie des Rechts*, in *Abhandlungen der Geistes—und Sozialwissenschaftlichen Klasse der Akademie der Wissenschaften und Literatur in Mainz*, 1961, No. 2, p. 90: 'Wir fragen, welchen strukturellen Erfordernissen Handlungen entsprechen müssen, wenn sie miteinander verträglich sein sollen; mit andern Worten, wir betrachten eine Welt, in der die Handelnden nicht miteinander kollidieren.'

18 Robert Frost in the poem 'Mending wall'.

19 John Milton, *The Tenure of Kings and Magistrates*, in *Works*, edited by R. Fletcher (London, 1838), p. 27: 'The power which is at the root of all liberty to dispose and economise in the land which God has given them, as masters of family in their own inheritance.'

20 Thomas Hobbes, *The Leviathan* (London, 1651), p. 91.

21 Montesquieu, *The Spirit of the Laws*, XVI, chapter 15.

22 J. Bentham, *The Theory of Legislation*, edited by C. K. Ogden (London, 1931), p. 113: 'Property and law are born together and must die together.'

23 Sir Henry Maine, *Village Communities* (London, 1880), p. 230: 'Nobody is at liberty to attack several property and to say at the same time that he values civilization. The history of the two cannot be disentangled.'

24 Lord Acton, *The History of Freedom* (London, 1907), p. 297: 'A people averse to the institution of private property is without the first elements of freedom.'

25 See A. I. Hallowell, 'Nature and function of property as a social institution', *Journal of Legal and Political Sociology*, i, 1943, p. 134:

From the standpoint of our contention that property rights of some kind are in fact not only universal but that they are a basic factor in the structuralization of the role of individuals in relation to basic economic processes, it is significant that eighteenth-century thinkers sensed the fundamental importance of property rights, even though their reasoning was on different lines from ours.

See also H. I. Hogbin, *Law and Order in Polynesia* (London, 1934), p. 77 *et seq.* and the introduction to this work by B. Malinowski, p. xli as well as the latter's *Freedom and Civilization* (London, 1944), pp. 132–3.

26 See in particular Immanuel Kant, *Metaphysik der Sitten*, in *Werke* (Akademie Ausgabe) vol. 6, pp. 382 and 396; and Mary J. Gregor, *Laws of Freedom* (Oxford, 1963).

27 David Hume, *Enquiry Concerning the Principles of Morals*, in *Essays* (London, 1875), vol. 2, p. 273.

28 Roscoe Pound, 'The theory of judicial decision', *Harvard Law Review*, ix, 1936, p. 52.

29 The most influential statement of this view is probably that by C. Beccaria, *On Crimes and Punishment* (1764), trans H. Paolucci (New York, 1963), p. 15: 'A judge is required to complete a perfect syllogism in which the major premise must be the general law, the minor the action that does or does not conform to the law; and the conclusion the acquittal or punishment.'

30 See Sir Alfred Denning, *Freedom under the Law* (London, 1949).

CHAPTER SIX THESIS: THE LAW OF LEGISLATION

* Paul A. Freund, 'Social justice and the law', in R. Brandt (ed), *Social Justice* (Englewood Cliffs, N.J., 1962), p. 94, and in the author's collection of essays *On Law and Justice* (Cambridge, Mass., 1968), p. 83. Compare with this J. W. Hurst, *Law and Social Process in U.S. History* (Ann Arbor, Mich., 1960), p. 5: 'Despite much contrary rhetoric our main operating philosophy has always been to use law to allocate resources positively to affect conditions of life where we saw something useful to be accomplished by doing so. . . . Law has meant organization for making and implementing choices among scarce resources of human satisfaction.'

On the Greek term *thesis* used in the title of this chapter (which corresponds to the German term *Satzung*) see John Burnet, 'Law and nature in Greek Ethics', *International Journal of Ethics*, vii, 1897, p. 332, where he shows that in contrast to *nomos*, which originally meant 'use', *thesis* 'may mean either the giving of law or the adoption of laws so given, and it thus contains the germ not only of the theory of the original legislator, but also that known as the Social Contract.'

1 See the famous statement by Edward Coke in 'Dr. Bonham's case', 8 Rep. 118a (1610): 'And it appears in our books, that in many cases, the Common Law will controul Acts of Parliament, and sometimes adjudge them to be utterly void: for when an Act of Parliament is

against common right and reason, or repugnant, or impossible to be performed, the Common Law will controul it, and adjudge such Act to be void.' For discussion of the significance of this case see C. H. McIlwain, *The High Court of Parliament* (New Haven, 1910); T. F. T. Plucknett, 'Bonham's case and judicial review', *Harvard Law Review*, xl, 1926–7; and S. E. Thorne, 'Bonham's case', *Law Quarterly Review*, liv, 1938. Even as late as 1766 William Pitt could still argue in the House of Commons (*Parliamentary History of England* (London, 1813), vol. 6, col. 195) that 'There are many things a parliament cannot do. It cannot make itself executive, nor dispose of offices which belong to the crown. It cannot take any man's property, even that of the meanest cottager, as in the case of enclosures, without his being heard.'

2 See J. C. Carter, *Law, Its Origin, Growth, and Function* (New York and London, 1907), p. 115: 'At the first appearance of legislation its province and the province of Public Law were nearly coterminous. The province of Private Law is scarcely touched.'

3 See Courtenay Ilbert, *Legislative Methods and Forms* (Oxford, 1901), p. 208: 'The English Legislature was originally constituted, not for legislative, but for financial purposes. Its primary function was, not to make laws, but to grant supplies.'

4 See J. C. Gray, *Nature and Sources of Law*, second edition (New York, 1921), p. 161: 'A statute is a general rule. A resolution by the legislature that a town shall pay one hundred dollars to Timothy Coggan is not a statute.'

5 Courtenay Ilbert, op. cit., p. 213.

6 See J. C. Carter, op. cit., p. 116:

> We find in the numerous volumes of statute books vast masses of matter which, though in the form of laws, are not laws in the proper sense. These consist in the making of provisions for the maintenance of public works of the State, for the building of asylums, hospitals, school-houses, and a great variety of similar matters. This is but the record of the actions of the State in relation to the *business* in which it is engaged. The State is a great public corporation which conducts a vast mass of business, and the written provisions for this, though in the form of laws, are not essentially different from the minutes or ordinary corporate bodies recording their actions . . . it is substantially true that the whole vast body of legislation is confined to Public Law and that its operation on Private Law is remote and indirect and aimed only to make the unwritten law of custom more easily and certainly enforced.

See also Walter Bagehot, *The English Constitution* (1967), World's Classics edition (Oxford, 1928), p. 10: 'The legislature chosen, in name, to make laws, in fact finds its principal business in making and keeping an executive'; and ibid., p. 119:

> An immense mass, indeed, of the legislation is not, in the proper language of jurisprudence, legislation at all. A law is a general command applicable to many cases. The 'special acts' which crowd the statute book and weary parliamentary committees are applicable to one case only. They do not lay down rules according to which railways shall be made, but enact that such and such a railway shall be made from this place to that place, and they have no bearing on any other transaction.

7 Courtenay Ilbert, op. cit., p. 6. See also ibid., p. 209 *et seq.*:

> When the authors of books on jurisprudence write about law, when professional lawyers talk about law, the kind of law about which they are mainly thinking is that which is found in Justinian's *Institutes*, or in the Napoleonic Codes, or in the New Civil Code of the German Empire, that is to say, the legal rules which relate to contracts and torts, to property, to family relations and inheritance, or else to law of crimes as is to be found in a Penal Code. They would also include the law of procedure, or 'adjective' law, to use a Benthamic term, in accordance with which substantive rules of law are administered by the courts. These branches of law make up what may perhaps be called 'lawyers' law.

8 See M. J. C. Vile, *Constitutionalism and the Separation of Powers* (Oxford, 1967); and W. B. Gwyn, *The Meaning of the Separation of Powers, Tulane Studies in Political Science*, IX (New Orleans, 1965). Gwyn shows that the idea of the separation of powers was inspired by three altogether different considerations which he labels the rule of law, and the accountability and the efficiency arguments. The rule of law argument would require that the legislature could pass only rules of just conduct equally binding on all private persons and on government. The accountability argument aims at making the small number of men who necessarily in fact conduct government responsible to the representative assembly, while the efficiency argument requires the delegation of the power of action to government because an assembly cannot efficiently conduct operations. It is obvious that on the second and on the third ground the assembly would be concerned also with government, but only in a supervisory or controlling capacity.

9 M. J. C. Vile, op. cit., p. 44.

10 *The First Agreement of the People of 28 October 1647*, in S. R. Gardiner, *History of the Great Civil War*, new edition (London, 1898), vol 3, p. 392.

11 [Marchamont Needham?], *A True Case of the Common Wealth* (London, 1654) quoted by M. J. C. Vile, op. cit., p. 10, where the book is

described as an 'official defence' of the *Instrument of Government of 1653.*

12 M. J. C. Vile, op. cit., p. 63: 'The power of legislation is itself limited to the exercise of its own proper functioning. John Locke's view was that the legislative authority is *to act in a particular way* . . . those who wield this authority should make *only* general rules. They are to govern by promulgated established Laws, not to be varied in particular cases.' See also ibid., pp. 214 and 217.

13 J. Bentham, *Constitutional Code*, in *Works*, IX, p. 119:

Why render the legislation omnicompetent? . . . Because it will better enable it to give effects to the will of the supreme constitutive, and advancement to the interest and security of the members of the state. . . . Because the practice upon which it puts an exclusion is, in a constitution such as the present, pregnant with evil in all imaginable shapes. Any limitation is in contradiction to the general happiness principle.

14 On the role of James Mill in this connection see M. J. C. Vile, op. cit., p. 217.

15 Robert A. Palmer, *The Age of Democratic Revolution*, vol 1, (Princeton, 1959).

16 The statement is quoted by J. Seeley, *Introduction to Political Science* (London, 1896), p. 216, but I have not been able to trace it in Napoleon's published correspondence.

17 G. W. F. Hegel, *Philosophie der Weltgeschichte* (quoted from the extracts in *Gesellschaft, Staat, Geschichte*, edited by F. Bülow, (Leipzig, 1931), p. 321):

Die erste Verfassung in Frankreich enthielt die absoluten Rechtsprinzipien in sich. Sie war die Konstituierung des Königtums; an der Spitze des Staates sollte der Monarch stehen, dem mit seinen Ministern die Ausübung zustehen sollte; der gesetzgebende Körper hingegen sollte die Gesetze machen. Aber diese Verfassung war sogleich ein innerer Widerspruch; denn die ganze Macht der Administration war in die gesetzgebende Gewalt verlegt: das Budget, Krieg und Frieden, die Aushebung der bewaffneten Macht kam der gesetzgebenden Körperschaft zu. Das Budget aber ist seinem Begriffe nach kein Gesetz, denn es wiederholt sich alle Jahre, und die Gewalt, die es zu machen hat, ist Regierungsgewalt. . . . Die Regierung wurde also in die Kammern verlegt wie in England in das Parlament.

18 W. Hasbach, *Die moderne Demokratie* (Jena, 1912), pp. 17 and 167.

19 See J. C. Carter, op. cit., p. 234: 'Legislative commands thus made, requiring special things to be done, are part of the machinery of government, but a part very different from that relating to the rules

which govern ordinary conduct of men in relation to each other. It is properly described as *public law*, by way of distinction from private law.' See also J. Walter Jones, *Historical Introduction to the Theory of Law* (Oxford, 1956), p. 146:

> There is e.g., the view that the essence of the State is the possession of supreme force. Public law, owing to its connection with the State, appears so strongly marked by the characteristic of force that the feature of order or regularity, which is so pronounced in the rules with which the lawyer is for the most part concerned, seems altogether overshadowed. In the result, the difference between public and private law becomes one of kind rather than of degree—a difference between force and rule. Public law ceases to be law at all, or at least to be law in the same sense as private law.
>
> At the opposite pole are found those lawyers who are primarily occupied with an independent science of public law. They have to recognize that it is too late in the day to deny that the rules grouped together as private law are entitled to the name of law, but far from regarding the association of the rules, forming the public law, with force, as a proof of their inferiority in comparison with private law, they see in it rather the mark of an inherent superiority. . . . The distinction therefore becomes one between relations of subordination and of co-ordination.

The clearest distinction between constitutional law as consisting of rules of organization and private law as of rules of conduct has been drawn by W. Burkhardt, *Einführung in die Rechtswissenschaft*, second edition (Zürich, 1948), especially p. 137:

> Der *erste* [der doppelten Gegensätze auf die die Gegenüberstellung von öffentlichen und privaten Recht zielt] beruht auf einer grundlegenden Verschiedenheit der Rechtsnormen: die *materiellen oder Verhaltensnormen* schreiben den Rechtsgenossen vor, was sie tun oder lassen sollen: die *formellen oder organisatorischen Normen* bestimmen, wie, d.h. durch wen und in welchem Verfahren, diese Regeln des Verhaltens gesetzt, angewendet und (zwangsweise) durchgesetzt werden. Die ersten kann man Verhaltensnormen, die zweiten Verfahrensnormen oder (i.w.S.) Verfassungsnormen nennen. Man nennt die ersten auch materielle, die zweiten formelle Normen. . . . Die ersten geben den Inhalt des Rechts, das rechtlich geforderte Verhalten, die zweiten entscheiden über seine Gültigkeit.

Burkhardt's distinction appears to have been accepted chiefly by other Swiss lawyers; see in particular Hans Nawiaski, *Allgemeine Rechtslehre als System der rechtlichen Grundbegriffe* (Zürich, 1948),

p. 265, and C. Du Pasquier, *Introduction à la théorie générale et la philosophie du droit*, third edition (Neuchatel, 1948), p. 49.

See, however, H. L. A. Hart, *The Concept of Law* (Oxford, 1961), p. 78:

> Under rules of one type, which may well be considered the basic or primary type, human beings are required to do or abstain from certain actions, whether they wish or not. Rules of the other type are in a sense parasitic or secondary on the first; for they provide that human beings may by doing or saying certain things introduce new rules of the primary type, extinguish or modify old ones, or in various ways determine their incidence or control their operations.

> See also Lon L. Fuller, *The Morality of Law* (New Haven, 1964), p. 63: 'Today there is a strong tendency to identify law, not with rules of conduct but with a hierarchy of power or command'; and ibid. p. 169, where he speaks of 'a confusion between law in the usual sense of rule of conduct directed toward the citizen, and government action generally'.

20 Ulpian, *Digests.* I,1,1,2, defines private law as *ius quod ad singulorum utilitatem spectat* and public law as *ius quod ad statum rei Romanae spectat*.

21 See Ernest Barker, *Principles of Social and Political Theory* (Oxford, 1951), p. 9: 'Some of it is primary or constitutional and some secondary or ordinary law.'

22 See J. E. M. Portalis, *Discours préliminaire du premier projet de code civil* (1801) in *Conference du Code Civil* (Paris, 1805), vol. 1, p. xiv: 'L'experience prouve que les hommes changent plus facilement le domination que de lois,'; See also H. Huber, *Recht, Staat und Gesellschaft* (Bern, 1954), p. 5: 'Staatsrecht vergeht, Privatrecht besteht.' Unfortunately, however, as Alexis de Tocqueville pointed out long ago, it is also true that constitutions pass, but administrative law persists.

23 H. L. A. Hart, op. cit.

24 Characteristic and most influential in the German literature in this respect is the criticism by A. Haenel, *Studien zum deutschen Staatsrecht, II. Das Gesetz im formellen und materiellen Sinn* (Leipzig, 1888), pp. 225–6, of E. Seligmann's definition of a *Rechtssatz* in *Der Begriff des Gesetzes im materiellen und formellen Sinn* (Berlin, 1886), p. 63, as a rule that 'abstrakt ist und eine nicht vorauszusehende Anzahl von Fällen ordnet', on the ground that this would exclude the fundamental rules of constitutional law. Indeed, it does, and the fathers of the American Constitution would probably have been horrified if it had been suggested that their handiwork was intended to be superior to the rules of just conduct as embodied in the common law.

25 See in particular Johannes Heckel, 'Einrichtung und rechtliche Bedeutung des Reichshaushaltgesetzes', *Handbuch des deutschen Staatsrechtes* (Tübingen, 1932), vol. 2, p. 390.

26 A. V. Dicey, *Lectures on the Relation between Law and Public Opinion in England during the Nineteenth Century* (London, 1903).

27 Rudolf Gneist, *Das englische Verwaltungsrecht der Gegenwart* (Berlin, 1883).

28 See in particular Walter Lippmann, *An Inquiry into the Principles of a Good Society* (Boston, 1937).

29 See E. Freund, *Administrative Powers over Persons and Property* (Chicago, 1928), p. 98.

30 Carl Schmitt, 'Legalität und Legitimität' (1932), reprinted in *Verfassungsrechtliche Aufsätze* (Berlin, 1958), p. 16.

31 Hans J. Morgenthau, *The Purpose of American Politics* (New York, 1960), p. 281: 'In our age, aside from still being the umpire, the state has also become the most powerful player, who, in order to make sure of the outcome, rewrites the rules of the game as he goes along.'

32 See Paul Vinogradoff, *Custom and Right* (Oslo, 1925), p. 10:

> The Trade Disputes Act of 1906 conferred on the unions an immunity from prosecution on the ground of tortious acts of their agents; this immunity stands in flagrant disagreement with the law of agency and the law as to companies represented by their officers in accordance with the Statutory Orders of 1883. The reason for this discordant state of the law is to be found in the resolve of legislation to secure for the unions a favourable position in their struggle with the employers.

See also the comments by A. V. Dicey, J. A. Schumpeter and Lord MacDermott quoted in F. A. Hayek, *The Constitution of Liberty* (London and Chicago, 1960), p. 504, note 3.

33 *Home Building and Loan Ass. v. Blaisdell*, 290 U.S. 398, 434, 444, 1934, according to which the state has 'authority to safeguard the vital interests of its people' and for this purpose to prevent 'the perversion of the [contract] clause through its use as an instrument to throttle the capacity of the States to protect their fundamental interests'.

34 Gustav Radbruch, 'Vom individualistischen Recht zum sozialen Recht' (1930), reprinted in *Der Mensch im Recht* (Göttingen, 1957), p. 40:

> Für eine individualistische Rechtsordnung ist das öffentliche Recht, ist der Staat nur der schmale schützende Rahmen, der sich um das Privatrecht und das Privateigentum dreht, für eine soziale Rechtsordnung ist umgekehrt das Privatrecht nur ein vorläufig ausgesparter und sich immer verkleinernder Spielraum

für die Privatinitiative innerhalb des all umfassenden öffentlichen Rechts.

35 Otto Mayer, *Deutsches Verwaltungsrecht*, vol 1. second edition (Munich and Leipzig, 1924), p. 14: 'Verwaltungsrecht ist das dem Verhaltniss zwischen dem verwaltenden Staate und den ihm dabei begegnenden Untertanen eigentumliche Recht.'
36 C. A. R. Crosland, *The Future of Socialism* (London, 1956), p. 205.

INDEX